Study Guide

to

Man, Economy, and State
A Treatise on Economic Principles

with

Power and Market
Government and the Economy

The Mises Institute dedicates this volume
in deepest gratitude to
Mr. Paul C. Reinhard.

Study Guide

to

Man, Economy, and State
A Treatise on Economic Principles

with

Power and Market
Government and the Economy

Scholar's Edition

Murray N. Rothbard

Robert P. Murphy

Ludwig von Mises Institute

AUBURN, ALABAMA

Copyright © 2006 by Ludwig von Mises Institute

All rights reserved. Written permission must be secured from the publisher to use or reproduce any part of this book, except for brief quotations in critical reviews or articles.

Published by the Ludwig von Mises Institute
518 West Magnolia Avenue, Auburn, Alabama 36832-4528.

ISBN-13: 978-1-933550-00-8
ISBN-10: 1-933550-00-7

CONTENTS

INTRODUCTION vii

MAN, ECONOMY, AND STATE

CHAPTER 1— FUNDAMENTALS OF HUMAN ACTION 1

CHAPTER 2— DIRECT EXCHANGE 15

CHAPTER 3— THE PATTERN OF INDIRECT EXCHANGE 27

CHAPTER 4— PRICES AND CONSUMPTION 39

CHAPTER 5— PRODUCTION: THE STRUCTURE 55

CHAPTER 6— PRODUCTION: THE RATE OF INTEREST
AND ITS DETERMINATION 69

CHAPTER 7— PRODUCTION: GENERAL PRICING
OF THE FACTORS 81

CHAPTER 8— PRODUCTION: ENTREPRENEURSHIP
AND CHANGE 93

v

CHAPTER 9— PRODUCTION: PARTICULAR FACTOR
PRICES AND PRODUCTIVE INCOMES 107

CHAPTER 10— MONOPOLY AND COMPETITION 121

CHAPTER 11— MONEY AND ITS PURCHASING POWER 135

CHAPTER 12— THE ECONOMICS OF VIOLENT
INTERVENTION IN THE MARKET 155

POWER AND MARKET

CHAPTER 1— DEFENSE SERVICES ON THE FREE MARKET . .175

CHAPTER 2— FUNDAMENTALS OF INTERVENTION 181

CHAPTER 3— TRIANGULAR INTERVENTION 189

CHAPTER 4— BINARY INTERVENTION: TAXATION 203

CHAPTER 5— BINARY INTERVENTION: GOVERNMENT
EXPENDITURES 219

CHAPTER 6— ANTIMARKET ETHICS: A PRAXEOLOGICAL
CRITIQUE 229

CHAPTER 7— CONCLUSION: ECONOMICS
AND PUBLIC POLICY .241

INDEX 249

INTRODUCTION

In June of 2004, I became convinced of the need for a study guide to accompany what is arguably the single most important book for the student of Austrian economics and libertarian policy analysis. Murray Rothbard's *Man, Economy, and State* is simply the most comprehensive exposition of Austrian economics that exists. Although Mises's *Human Action* is itself a self-contained, beautiful work of sheer brilliance, it is nonetheless the case that, in his subsequent work, Rothbard *teaches economics* more clearly. *Power and Market* builds on the analysis of *Man, Economy, and State* to provide an exhaustive classification and critique of government intervention in all of its various forms. Originally intended as a single volume, *Man, Economy, and State* and *Power and Market* were published separately due to (alleged) space constraints and, no doubt, the radical positions contained in the latter. The Mises Institute's lovely Scholar's Edition has reunited these two works as Rothbard meant them to be. However, I shall omit further discussion of the publication background (inasmuch as a historical sketch is provided in Joseph Stromberg's Introduction to the scholar's edition) and explain the format of this study guide.

The chapters of this guide match the twelve of *Man, Economy, and State* and the seven of *Power and Market*; appendices

vii

viii   *Study Guide to Man, Economy, and State with Power and Market*

are handled within each chapter. A typical chapter[1] begins with a one-page summary. This is then followed by a detailed outline of the chapter, which follows Rothbard's format (Arabic numerals, then English letters, etc.) for sections and subsections. (The length of Rothbard's chapter consequently influences the length of the detailed outline in the study guide.) Following the detailed outline are the "contributions" of the chapter. Sometimes these observations refer to techniques or doctrines that are unique to the Austrian School, while at other times they refer to innovations engineered by Rothbard himself. (This distinction is always made clear.) The next section contains the technical details, intended for advanced readers (in particular graduate students). Generally, in this section I contrasted Rothbard's approach with mainstream economics, but I also (especially for chapters from *Power and Market*) would sometimes consider objections that Rothbard had not, or would simply take a given discussion a little further than he had done in the text.

Finally, each chapter of the study guide contains ten questions. Some of the questions merely test reading comprehension; they ensure that the conscientious (but perhaps intimidated and/or overwhelmed) reader is absorbing the important points. However, especially to challenge the more advanced readers, some of the questions take an *advocatus diaboli* approach and point to ostensible contradictions or problems with Rothbard's analysis. (Whether the reader can resolve the alleged flaws or not, he or she will undoubtedly understand Rothbard's case much more after considering these questions.) Where

---

[1]I say "typical" because some chapters in *Power and Market* are so short that their corresponding treatments in this study guide contain merely the summary or the detailed outline.

Introduction   *ix*

appropriate, I have included the relevant page numbers (from the scholar's edition) after each question to save the reader time.

I strongly urge all those who take Austrian economics seriously to read (at least large portions of) Rothbard's treatise; I would go so far as to say that a modern academic cannot really call him or herself an Austrian economist without doing so. For those who may be intimidated or discouraged by the massive volume, I hope that this study guide will at least "chart the territory" and allow them to begin in those topics that most interest them. At that point, I suspect, Rothbard's spell will overtake them and they will be compelled to read all 1,441 pages.

Let me end this brief introduction by urging even older experts to reread this important book. I myself had read *Man, Economy, and State* cover to cover in college, and yet I was *amazed* at how much better it had grown over the years! In addition, I hope that this study guide may provide a useful reference for such experts. (I myself have used it to refresh my memory on a particularly subtle aspect of Rothbard's approach to capital and growth.)

Enough now with the introduction. . . . The reader must open the treatise and let the learning begin!

ROBERT P. MURPHY
January 2006

CHAPTER 1

FUNDAMENTALS OF HUMAN ACTION

Chapter Summary

Praxeology is the scientific study of human action, which is *purposeful behavior*. A human acts whenever he uses *means* to achieve an end that he or she subjectively values. Human action is thus teleological or intentional; a person acts for a *reason*. Therefore not all human behavior is action in the praxeological sense: purely reflexive or unconscious bodily movements (such as coughing when exposed to tear gas) are not examples of action. Praxeology starts from the undeniable axiom that human beings exist and act, and then logically deduces implications of this fact. These deduced propositions are true *a priori*; there is no need to test them in the way that a physicist might test a proposed "law" of Nature. So long as a praxeological statement has been derived correctly, it must necessarily contain as much truth as the original axioms.

All action involves an *exchange*, or a *choice*: the actor attempts to achieve a more satisfactory state of affairs than what would have occurred had the actor chosen differently. The benefit of an action is its *psychic revenue*, while its cost is the value the actor places on the next-best alternative. Each actor can arrange various possible ends on a *scale of value*. This is a purely ordinal ranking, that can only show which end *is* first-best, second-best, and so forth. There is no sense in saying that one end is 8

1

percent better than another, because there is no cardinal unit of happiness.

Every action involves not only a value judgment concerning different ends, but also a *belief* on the part of the actor that he possesses adequate means to achieve his desired end. (A person may prefer sunshine to rain, but this preference alone will not lead to any action if the person does not believe he has the power to change the weather.)

Only individuals can act, because only individuals have valuations and can make choices. It is thus metaphorical to say that "the people elected the president" or "Germany attacked France." Of course, individuals may act in a particular way because of political ideas or because military generals gave certain orders; nonetheless it is always *individuals* who act.

All action takes place in time. We can define the time *before* a given action, the *duration* of the action, and the time *after* a given action. All action is future-oriented, in the sense that action seeks to create a more desirable future from the actor's viewpoint. All individuals possess *time preference*, which means that they prefer a given satisfaction sooner rather than later.

Individuals make decisions *on the margin*. No one ever chooses between "diamonds" and "water." Rather, an individual must choose between a definite amount of diamonds and a definite amount of water.

All action involves *uncertainty* of the future. (If the future were completely known and hence determined, there would be no scope for action.) *Entrepreneurship* involves coping with this uncertainty by forecasting future conditions, and hence is implicit in every action.

Chapter 1: Fundamentals of Human Action   *3*

Chapter Outline

1. The Concept of Action

The distinctive feature of the study of man is *action*, which is *purposeful behavior*. (A falling rock is not "acting" because it doesn't "wish" to get closer to the ground.) But the social scientist (including the economist) must impute subjective intentions to the objects of his study (i.e., acting human beings). Action must exist; if beings did not behave purposefully, they would not be human.

Praxeology is the scientific study of action. It begins with the obvious truth that action exists, because human beings exist. (If things did not behave purposefully, so that the observer could ascribe motives to the things, then they would not be classified as human.) Praxeology consists of all the propositions that can be logically derived from the action axiom. Economics is the best developed subdivision of praxeology. (NOTE: Some economic propositions require supplementary assumptions besides the action axiom.)

2. First Implications of the Concept

Only individuals can act. When people say things such as, "The group went to the park," or "Germany attacked France," this is really just a shorthand for saying that certain *individuals* performed these actions. This is purely a methodological point; it does not (as many critics falsely assert) mean that economists deny the existence of social collectives, or that economists think individuals always behave "atomistically." Of course, a person may act differently when he is in a mob. But nonetheless even "mob behavior" is still the sum total of the behavior of each individual comprising the "mob." A chemist can say that all matter is composed of atoms without thereby denying the existence of molecules.

A person will act only if he desires a particular state of affairs *and* only if he believes he has the capacity to bring this about. For example, a man may desire sunshine on a cloudy day, but this desire alone will not lead to any action, because the man has no idea how to change the weather.

A man uses *means* to (attempt to) achieve his ends. When a man uses a certain means for one end, then he cannot use it for some other possible end; we thus say that the means is *scarce*. In contrast, if a particular item or condition is so abundant that man is not faced with a choice in its disposal, then it is not a means but a *general condition* of the environment. (For example, air is certainly necessary for action, but we would not normally classify it as a means to an end.)

All action takes place *in time*. For any given action, we can conceive of the time before the action, the time absorbed by the action, and the time following the action. Time is scarce. The future itself is uncertain, and hence acting man must engage in *entrepreneurship* by *speculating* about future conditions and the results of various possible actions.

Acting man must rank the possible ends in order of desirability. Because means are scarce, acting man must allocate them to fulfill his most highly ranked ends; i.e., acting man must *economize* the means. Even though a man will always dispose of his means in an attempt to achieve his most highly ranked ends, because of uncertainty the man may err.

3. Further Implications: The Means

The means to satisfy wants are called *goods*. Those goods that directly satisfy wants are *consumers' goods* or *goods of the first order*. Those goods that are useful only indirectly in satisfying wants are *producers' goods* or *factors of production* or *goods of higher order*. (These terms are interchangeable, depending on the context.) If a ham sandwich is the consumers' good, then the loaf of bread, labor of the housewife (in making the sandwich), and the unsliced ham would all be *first-order producers' goods*. Goods which are involved in the production of *these* goods (perhaps the labor of the store clerk in selling the loaf of bread) would be *second-order producers' goods*, and so forth.

The two *original* factors of production are *labor* and *land*. (*Land* is a technical term that includes not only land in the popular sense, but all natural resources, such as deposits of copper.) In addition to these factors we also have *capital goods*, which are factors of production that are themselves *produced* by human beings (with labor, land, and possibly other capital goods). Notice that all capital goods can ultimately be traced back to the input of the original factors, land and labor.

The value of producers' goods derives from the value that acting man places on the final, consumers' goods that they produce. In our example above, the loaf of bread is valuable because it contributes to the production of the ham sandwich.

4. Further Implications: Time

The time elapsing from the beginning of an action until the end is achieved is the *period of production*. The period of production is the *working time* plus the *maturing time*. Note that the period of production for a given consumer good does *not* include the time used in the construction of all capital goods used in the process. Although the economist must distinguish between original and produced factors, acting man does not care about the past; he takes the supplies of labor, land, and presently available (i.e., previously produced) capital goods as a given when he forms his plans.

All people prefer a *given end* to be achieved sooner rather than later. This is the universal fact of *time preference*. Apparent counterexamples to this law are due to confusion over the nature of a good. For example, if a person in the winter prefers "future ice" to "present ice," this does not violate the law of time preference, because ice-in-the-summer is a different good from ice-in-the-winter.

5. Further Implications

A. Ends and Values

All action aims at exchanging a less satisfactory state of affairs for a more satisfactory state. We can say that individuals rank outcomes in terms of happiness, utility, satisfaction, contentment, etc. Regardless of the name, these terms are purely formal, and do not imply hedonism or crude Benthamite utilitarianism.

Value rankings are always *ordinal*, never *cardinal*. There is no unit of happiness or utility, and hence we can only say that a man preferred A to B; we can never say he preferred A "three times as much."

B. The Law of Marginal Utility

Each unit of a good is valued separately. People never choose between "guns" or "butter" but rather between a *unit* of guns and a *unit* of butter. The total *supply* or *stock* of a good is defined by units that are equally serviceable, or interchangeable, from the actor's point of view.

As an actor acquires more and more units of a good, he devotes them to successively less and less urgent ends (i.e., ends that are lower on his scale of values). Therefore the *marginal utility* of a good declines as its supply increases. This is the law of *diminishing marginal utility*.

Chapter 1: Fundamentals of Human Action   7

6. Factors of Production: The Law of Returns

Units of producers' goods are also evaluated on the margin. The value assigned to a unit of a producers' good is the value of the consumers' goods that would be lost if the marginal unit of the producers' good in question were no longer available. (This is the *marginal product* of the factor of production.)

The factors of production necessary to produce a certain consumer good are called *complementary factors of production*. The *law of returns* states that with the quantity of complementary factors held constant, there always exists some optimum amount of the varying factor.

7. Factors of Production: Convertibility and Valuation

Factors of production differ in their degree of *specificity*, i.e., the variety of consumers' goods that they can produce. Labor is completely *nonspecific*, because it is used in the production of every consumers' good. The less specific a factor is, the more *convertible* it is when conditions change and plans must be altered.

8. Factors of Production: Labor versus Leisure

Throughout the book we assume that human beings find labor onerous; i.e., we assume that individuals value *leisure* as a consumer good.

9. The Formation of Capital

Capital goods can be produced only through the act of *saving*, i.e., consuming less in the present than one's means allow. We can imagine Robinson Crusoe on his desert island, able to pick berries with his bare hands. If Crusoe *invests* some of his labor, not on immediate consumption (i.e., picking berries), but rather on the creation of capital goods such as a stick, then he can increase his future consumption of berries. This would be a "roundabout" method of picking berries; in general these methods are more physically productive than shorter, more direct methods. An actor will opt for longer, more roundabout methods so long as the enhanced output more than offsets the increased waiting time, which in itself is a disadvantage because of time preference.

Chapter 1: Fundamentals of Human Action   9

Notable Contributions

• The Misesian scheme of *praxeology* is a unique feature of the Austrian School. Whereas other schools of thought (to the extent that they even concern themselves with methodology at all) embrace some form of positivism or institutionalism, the Austrians are unique in stressing the *a priori*, deductive nature of economic law.

• The *structure of production* concept is also a particularly Austrian feature. By classifying goods as first-, second-, third-order, and so on, the Austrians never lose sight of the fact that *production takes time*. The ordering of goods in this fashion goes back to Menger, but it was Böhm-Bawerk who fully elaborated the role of savings and capital accumulation. Mainstream economists, such as J.B. Clark and Frank Knight, downplayed the role of production time in modern economies. They would argue that if a production process is fully "synchronized," such that inputs in the highest stages correspond to output emerging from the other end, then there is no apparent time lag between investment and consumption. (Of course, this is only true in a stationary state.)

• The use of "Robinson Crusoe" scenarios, although popular in earlier economic treatises, has come under fire for being "unrealistic." The Austrians continue to stress the importance of the study of isolated man to discover *a priori* truths that are useful in the study of man in society.

• There is a subtle difference between the philosophical position of Rothbard and Mises. In *Human Action*,

Mises says that man acts to remove "felt uneasiness." Rothbard, in contrast, merely says that man acts to achieve a more satisfactory state of affairs (i.e., Rothbard's position is not as "pessimistic").

Chapter 1: Fundamentals of Human Action *11*

Technical Matters

1. One must distinguish between marginal product and the *value of* marginal product. Rothbard writes correctly that "the value assigned to a unit of a factor of production is equal to the *value of its marginal product*, or its *marginal productivity*" (p. 34). In formal economics you may often see, e.g., the marginal product of labor defined as the derivative of the production function with respect to labor, i.e., how much more physical product will accrue if the firm hires one more unit of labor. But this definition is a physical one, not one based on *value*. The value of the labor is the *value* placed on this increment in physical output.

2. Strictly speaking, it is imprecise to define capital goods as "produced factors of production." In Austrian theory, the purpose for classifying goods as capital versus original is that, in the ERE, only the original factors earn *net* rents. Capital goods, in contrast, earn only a *gross* return; their rental payments exactly correspond to the payments for the factors used in their construction (due account being made for interest). Consequently, the better definition of a capital good would be a *reproducible* factor of production, in contrast with an original factor, which is *nonreproducible*. (See Rothbard's Introduction to Frank A. Fetter's *Capital, Interest, and Rent*.)

3. Although Rothbard's discussion of the ham sandwich (pp. 8–9) is a useful introduction to

the concept of stages of production, even
here the classification of goods ultimately
relies on the subjective plans of individuals.
There is not an objective "fact of the matter"
about the order (first-, second-, third-, etc.)
in which a certain good should be placed.
The classification depends upon the means-
end framework as conceived by the relevant
individual.

Chapter 1: Fundamentals of Human Action   *13*

Study Questions

1. If an infant cries immediately after birth, is this action in the praxeological sense? What if the infant, several months later, has learned that crying will often lead to attention from parents? (pp. 1–2)

2. When doctors in the 1800s used leeches in an attempt to help patients, was this an example of human action? (p. 7)

3. Suppose a man is strumming his guitar while sitting on the sidewalk in a large city, and that his only purpose is to listen to the enjoyable music. How should the guitar be classified? What if passersby begin giving the man loose change, so that he now views the guitar as a means to earning money? (pp. 8–9)

4. Suppose that a boy, on June 4, is offered the choice of seeing a fireworks show that day, or in exactly one month. If the boy chooses the show in the future, has he violated the law of time preference? (pp. 15–16)

5. Suppose someone says, "I like steak more than burgers, and I like burgers more than hot dogs, but my preference for steak over burgers is definitely stronger than my preference for burgers over hot dogs." What do you think Rothbard would say about this statement? (pp. 18–19)

6. Imagine that a chemist measures two bottles of water, and finds that the first contains 8.002 ounces of water, while the second bottle contains 8.001 ounces of water. The chemist concludes that the bottles of water are definitely different objects. How should the economist treat them? (p. 23)

7. What are the two ways that capital increases productivity? (p. 48)

8. What are the definitions of *consumption, saving,* and *investment*? (pp. 48, 53)

9. If capital goods increase the productivity of labor, why don't people create as many capital goods as possible? (pp. 48–49)

10. Suppose that a farmer normally sets aside 10 percent of his harvest as seed corn. His son says, "That's silly! We should sell all of our harvest and make as much money as possible." What would this policy lead to? (p. 55)

CHAPTER 2

DIRECT EXCHANGE

Chapter Summary

Direct exchange involves trades where the goods received are of *direct use to the recipient*. These "direct uses" can be for production; i.e., a person can engage in direct exchange of higher-order goods. However, if a person desires a good with the intention to trade it away to someone else, then he is engaged in *indirect exchange*, the subject of the next chapter.

A voluntary exchange involves a *reverse valuation* of the goods: each party values what he is giving up less than what he is receiving in exchange. This principle underscores the fact that value is subjective: if goods had an objective, intrinsic value, then there could be no reverse valuation (except through error). If this were the case, then traded goods would be equal in value (and hence there would be no reason to trade them), or one party would necessarily benefit at the expense of the other. But since this is *not* the case—i.e., since individuals value goods differently—then there are mutual "gains from trade." Both parties (expect to) benefit from a voluntary exchange.

With the possibility of trade, goods are valued not only by their direct *use-value* but also their *exchange-value*. An actor will always value a unit of a good at the higher of these two. (For example, even a nonsmoker would prefer a box of cigars over a hot dog, if he thought he could trade the former to a smoker.) Trade also fosters *specialization* and the *division of*

15

labor. By specializing in those activities in which they are relatively most productive (or have the *comparative advantage*), actors greatly increase the productivity of their labor and enjoy more consumption goods than would be possible without trade.

The *price* of one good in terms of another is the number of units of the second good that must be offered in exchange for one unit of the first good. Other things equal, a seller prefers the highest price possible while a buyer prefers the lowest price possible.

Individuals enter a market seeking to exchange goods they value less for goods they value more. There is scope for trade whenever the *minimum selling price* of the seller is lower than the *maximum buying price* of the buyer. The market *supply* relates the quantity of goods that will be offered at various prices, while the market *demand* relates the quantity of goods that buyers will attempt to purchase at various prices. The *equilibrium price* is that which equates quantity supplied with quantity demanded. There is a tendency for actual market prices to approach equilibrium, but new changes in the data constantly interrupt this tendency. *Speculation* (if successful) speeds the move to equilibrium.

In an unhampered market (i.e., one free from violence and theft), all property can be traced back through voluntary exchanges, production, and ultimately to the original appropriation of raw (unowned) land.

Chapter 2: Direct Exchange 17

Chapter Outline

1. Types of Interpersonal Action: Violence

The analysis of chapter 1 was true for all action, but its *applications* were limited to isolated individuals (i.e., autistic exchange). Praxeology is now used to analyze interpersonal action (i.e., interpersonal exchange).

When one person increases his own satisfaction by using another person as a factor of production against the latter's will, we can say that the former person is exploiting the latter. Such a *hegemonic* relationship stands in contrast to voluntary arrangements. By definition, a slave does not benefit from his relationship with his master. If the slave *agreed* that he benefited (in terms of relatively reliable food, shelter, etc. in exchange for labor), then coercion would not be necessary to maintain the relationship.

2. Types of Interpersonal Action: Voluntary Exchange and the Contractual Society

Unless stated otherwise, the remainder of the book assumes that all exchanges are voluntary, i.e., no one violates the property of anyone else. (This includes the property in one's body.) The analysis is therefore of an *unhampered market*.

Individuals will engage in an exchange only if they have a *reverse valuation* of the goods *and* if they are aware of each other. To understand the first condition, suppose that Smith trades one apple to Jones in exchange for one orange. Because the transaction is voluntary, it must be the case that Smith values the orange more highly than the apple, while Jones must value the apple more highly than the orange. Notice that this alone will not lead to a trade; Smith and Jones must be aware of each other's existence.

In general, an individual will be willing to trade away units of some good X in exchange for units of some other good Y, so long as the marginal utility of Y is higher than the marginal utility of X. Notice that as more units are swapped, the marginal utility of X rises while the marginal utility of Y falls.

The possibility of exchange with others means that an actor will now consider not only the direct *use-value* of a good but also its *exchange-value*. The marginal utility of a given unit of a good is the higher of these two (i.e., a person will continue to trade away units of a good so long as the exchange-value of the marginal unit is higher than the use-value). Because of diminishing marginal utility, owners of large stocks of goods (such as people producing for a market) usually consider the exchange-value more relevant.

A helpful outline of the types of human action is presented on page 94.

3. Exchange and the Division of Labor

The opportunities for exchange lead to *specialization* and the *division of labor*. This allows for more consumption for everyone involved. If we consider that each market participant has an *absolute* advantage in the production of a certain good, then it is obvious that specialization will allow for higher total output (and hence consumption per capita). However, even if one market participant has an absolute advantage in every line of production, he can still benefit by specializing in the product in which he has the *comparative* (or *relative*) advantage.

4. Terms of Exchange

The *price* of a good in terms of another is simply the number of units of the second good that must be offered in order to receive one unit of the first good in exchange. Although we are used to quoting prices in terms of money, this need not be the

Chapter 2: Direct Exchange

case. For example, if a person can trade two cows for 1,000 berries, then the "berry-price" of one cow is 500 berries.

Other things equal, a seller will always prefer a higher price for his goods and a buyer will always prefer a lower price. Apparent counterexamples (such as someone selling a car to an in-law at a lower price than could be gotten from a stranger) are not comparing the same goods.

5. Determination of Price: Equilibrium Price

A sale can occur when the *minimum selling price of the seller* is lower than the *maximum buying price of the buyer*. These minimum and maximum prices can be determined from the value scales of the individuals in the market. If there are only two individuals, usually there will be a *range* of possible prices. Praxeology alone cannot say which particular price will be used; it depends on the relative bargaining skill of the individuals. With the addition of more and more buyers and sellers to the market, the zone of indeterminacy shrinks, so that only a few (or possibly one) price will "clear the market."

The *demand* for a good indicates the quantity of units that buyers desire at various hypothetical prices. The *supply* of a good indicates the quantity of units that sellers offer at various hypothetical prices. These can be depicted in a table (or *schedule*) or plotted as a graph (or *curve*). One must distinguish between a change in demand (movement *of* the demand curve) versus a change in *quantity* demanded (movement *along* a given demand curve), and the same for supply.

An *equilibrium price* is one in which quantity supplied equals quantity demanded. Graphically, it occurs at the intersection of the supply and demand curves. The market tends toward equilibrium: If the current price is above the equilibrium price, there is an excess supply ("surplus") and sellers reduce their asking price. If the current price is below the equilibrium price, there is an excess demand ("shortage") and buyers increase their offer price.

There is a tendency for *one price* to rule over a market. If there weren't, then arbitrage opportunities would exist; a middleman could buy low and sell high.

6. Elasticity of Demand

The elasticity of demand is the ratio of the percentage change in quantity demanded and the percentage change in price (the negative sign is omitted). If the elasticity is greater than one, the demand for the good is "elastic," while if the elasticity is less than one the demand is "inelastic." Note that a higher price will lead to lower total spending on a good if its demand is elastic, while a higher price will lead to higher total spending if the demand is inelastic.

7. Speculation and Supply and Demand Schedules

Supply and demand take into account all factors influencing people's selling and buying decisions. In particular, someone may refuse to sell a good at a certain price, because he speculates that the price of the good will rise in the near future. Or, a buyer may refrain from purchasing a good, because he *speculates* that the price will soon fall. Such speculation (if correct) "flattens" the supply and demand curves, and speeds the approach towards equilibrium.

8. Stock and the Total Demand to Hold

Rather than analyzing traditional supply and demand, we may also understand price formation using the concepts of *total stock* and *total demand to hold*. The stock of a good is the number of units existing at any given time. The total demand to hold consists of the number of units desired by buyers, *plus* the

Chapter 2: Direct Exchange

number of units that current owners *refrain* from selling (what is called the *reservation demand*). The equilibrium price equates the stock and the total demand to hold.

One drawback of this approach is that it obscures the volume of exchange in a market; one cannot tell if the people ending up with units of the good are the same as the ones who started out with them. However, the approach is very useful in illustrating that ultimately supply and demand are *both* determined by utility considerations, rather than "real cost."

9. Continuing Markets and Changes in Price

In the real world, markets are continually upset by changes in the data. Production and consumption can be handled using the appropriate shifts in the supply of a good.

10. Specialization and Production of Stock

With specialization, the use-value of goods to their original owners declines. In practice, a producer's reservation demand is purely speculative, i.e., the producer will only refrain from selling at the current price if he or she believes a higher price will obtain in the future.

11. Types of Exchangeable Goods

The principles of supply and demand explain price formation for any type of good, whether tangible commodities, services, or claims. (A partial outline of the possible exchanges is listed on page 163 and is completed on pages 168–69.)

12. Property: The Appropriation of Raw Land

In an unhampered market, the origin of all property is traceable to voluntary exchanges and ultimately to the appropriation of unowned nature-given factors. An actor legitimately *homesteads* a piece of previously unowned land by "mixing his labor" with it. Note that a person does not need to *continually* "use" a piece of land, once he has established ownership.

13. Enforcement Against Invasion of Property

This section analyzes the precise meaning of an "unhampered market" (the major subject of study in the book) by defining what is, and what is not, a violation of property rights.

Chapter 2: Direct Exchange

Notable Contributions

• Unlike the positivist, model-building approach of the mainstream, Austrian economics seeks to explain the formation of *actual market prices* in the *real world*.

• Figure 7 (p. 99) helps the reader visualize specialization under barter.

• Rothbard follows Mises (pp. 100–01) by arguing that feelings of community and altruism are the result (not the cause) of social cooperation and the higher productivity made possible by the division of labor.

• The depictions of value scales are extremely helpful in the analysis of price formation.

• Rothbard's discussion of property rights in the radio spectrum and waterways (pp. 173–74) was quite advanced for its day.

• Packed into the section, "Enforcement Against Invasion of Property" (pp. 176–85), Rothbard offers unorthodox (and perhaps shocking) insights on issues such as fraud, negotiable instruments, externalities, libel and slander, and blackmail.

24   *Study Guide to Man, Economy, and State with Power and Market*

Technical Matters

1.   Some of the conditions claimed sufficient for an exchange are only strictly true if we rule out errors in bargaining ploys. For example, on page 86 Rothbard says that a reverse valuation between A and B over a vase and a typewriter, plus the mutual awareness of the assets, will lead to an exchange. But it is possible that B might insist on a vase *plus* 10 berries (say), thinking that A will agree to this. If A calls B's bluff, then it is possible that no trade will occur, despite the reverse valuations and awareness of the assets.

2.   The literal case of "log-rolling" (pp. 101–02) illustrates a subtle point concerning the division of labor. Certain tasks require the cooperation of several individuals (such as rolling logs or moving furniture). Cooperation raises the productivity of each participant's labor. However, this is not a case of specialization or the division of labor, since each participant is performing the same type of labor. Rather than considering two neighbors helping each other move couches, a better example of specialization would be one neighbor doing the yard work for both while the second neighbor replaces the gutters on both houses.

3.   In footnote 20 (p. 102), Rothbard says that specialization in a particular *stage* of production (rather than in a consumption good) requires "the adoption of *indirect* exchange, discussed in the following chapters." Recall that under direct exchange, each individual seeks to attain goods that he or she can actually use (rather than merely to trade away to other individuals). Therefore, it is impossible under direct

Chapter 2: Direct Exchange   *25*

exchange for people to specialize in particular stages of production, because (by definition) higher order goods are not suitable for immediate consumption. If everyone specializes in one stage, then Smith (who mines ore) can have at most one buyer, Jones (who smelts ore). But Smith can't directly use the smelted ore that Jones has to offer, because Smith (by assumption) specializes in mining.

4.   An individual always seeks to maximize his psychic revenue (p. 104), *not* his psychic profit. Remember that value rankings are always ordinal. It would make no sense to gauge the "difference" in utility between the first and second most highly ranked uses for a good (and hence to try to measure the psychic profit).

5.   Figure 15 (p. 123) may confuse the reader because it apparently ranks additional horses higher on the actor's value scale. However, as the text makes clear, these are successive horses that could be *sold*. Thus, if the actor initially possesses ten horses, then we could replace "A horse," "A second horse," and so on with, "Nine horses," "Eight horses," etc.

6.   Although Rothbard disparages the practice in footnote 27 (p. 130), the "elasticity of supply" can be defined even without resort to calculus; it is simply the percentage change in quantity supplied divided by the percentage change in price. Many mainstream economists use this concept to study such things as the relative burden of excise taxes. They could also say that speculation causes the supply curve in figure 20 (p. 132) to become more elastic, just as Rothbard says that speculation causes the demand curve in figure 19 to become more elastic.

26   *Study Guide to Man, Economy, and State with Power and Market*

Study Questions

1. Do different praxeological laws apply to situations of isolation versus society? (p. 79)

2. What is Rothbard's definition of *society*? (p. 84)

3. Give an example of *autistic exchange*. (p. 84)

4. Suppose someone says, "In order for an exchange to be just, each person must give up an equal value for an equal value." What do you think Rothbard would say about this? (p. 85)

5. What are three sources of ownership? (p. 93)

6. What is the law of association? How does it relate to Boulding's example of the doctor and his gardener? (p. 98)

7. In figure 16, how many horses will Smith demand at a price of 85 berries? At that price, how many total berries will Smith offer in exchange? (p. 125)

8. What will happen to the price if the total demand to hold is higher than the stock? (pp. 137–40)

9. How can the principles of this chapter be applied to shares of ownership? (p. 166)

10. What is Rothbard's response to Henry George? (pp. 171–72)

CHAPTER 3

THE PATTERN OF INDIRECT EXCHANGE

Chapter Summary

Although beneficial to all participants, the scope of direct exchange is very limited. Unless there is a "coincidence of wants"—where Paul wants to obtain and use X and is willing to give up Y for it, while Mary wants to obtain and use Y and is willing to give up X for it—direct exchange cannot occur. Under direct exchange, there is little room for the division of labor and capitalistic production processes.

Indirect exchange occurs when at least one of the parties obtains a good that he does *not* intend to directly use in consumption or production, but rather that he intends to eventually trade away to someone else. This good would then be a *medium of exchange*. In principle, there can be many different types of media of exchange in an economy, each of which is used as a medium only by a few people. However, if a particular good is a medium of exchange that is *commonly accepted* (i.e., everyone is willing to accept this good in the hope of trading it away again in the future), then that good is a *money*.

The emergence of money is a market phenomenon, resulting from the actions of self-interested individuals. Even in an initial state of *barter*, commodities will have different degrees of *marketability*, or *saleability*. Consequently, sellers of relatively unmarketable commodities may often find it advantageous to

28   Study Guide to Man, Economy, and State with Power and Market

proceed "indirectly" by selling their wares, not against the commodities they ultimately desire (and for which they can find no owners who at the same time desire the unmarketable wares), but in exchange for commodities that they can't use personally, but which are at least more marketable than the initial commodities being sold. This indirect route will put these sellers in a much better position to obtain the commodities that they ultimately desire for personal use (in consumption or production).

Because relatively more marketable commodities will be demanded, not merely on account of their intrinsic usefulness, but also because people will desire them as media of exchange, such commodities will become acceptable by ever more people, and hence they will grow even *more* marketable. The process builds on itself, until eventually one or more commodities become generally accepted media of exchange, i.e., money. A money commodity tends to be highly divisible, easy to transport, durable, and has a convenient exchange value per unit weight. Historically, gold and silver have often served as money.

The unit of money is typically expressed as a weight, as in *pounds* of silver or *ounces* of gold. The particular unit used is a matter of convenience, however.

The emergence of money allows for a fuller division of labor and extension of roundabout processes. Economic calculation becomes possible, as all goods are now traded against the money good and can hence be reduced to a common denominator. Businesspeople can now compare money revenues with money expenditures and obtain a quantitative appraisal of their operations. Profit and loss calculations allow businesses to evaluate the successfulness of various departments or projects.

Catallactics is the branch of praxeology that deals with monetary exchange ratios.

Chapter Outline

1. The Limitations of Direct Exchange

Although direct exchange allows all participants to achieve greater satisfaction than would be possible in autarky, it is nonetheless quite limited. Recall that in direct exchange, each party gives up goods in order to receive goods that he or she can *personally* use (either in consumption or production). Therefore, unless there is a "coincidence of wants"—where Paul wants to obtain and use X and is willing to give up Y for it, while Mary wants to obtain and use Y and is willing to give up X for it—two people cannot engage in direct exchange.

This fact poses a serious limitation on the scope of direct exchange, and would greatly hamper the division of labor. For example, someone couldn't specialize and become a full-time dentist, unless he were confident that, whenever he desired apples or water or a horse, he would be able to (quickly) find an owner of apples, water, or horses who *at that time* desired dental services. For a different example, consider the owner of an indivisible but very valuable good, such as a famous work of art. It is unlikely that the owner would ever sell this item, because she would need to find someone who had a combination of various other goods (such as steaks, a motorcycle, china) that the art owner desired, *and* who wanted to trade this package of goods for that particular piece of art. What are the chances of finding such a person?

Finally, consider the limitations on extended production. How could the builder of houses possibly operate using only direct exchange? Unless he happened to find himself in possession of a giant stockpile of just the right assortment of various goods to pay workers and the owners of lumber, shingles, nails, etc., he would not even be able to construct a house in the first place. (Remember that it would be impermissible for the

30   Study Guide to Man, Economy, and State with Power and Market

builder to go out on the market and *accumulate* such a stockpile. Since the builder would be acquiring these various goods with the intention of trading them away to workers and other factor owners, this would already constitute an example of *indirect* exchange.) After the house were completed, the builder would then be in the same unfortunate position as the owner of a famous piece of art: he would have to find a buyer who had an acceptable stockpile of goods that the *builder* desired, and who at the same time wanted to trade them for the house. Clearly, an economy characterized only by direct exchange would have an extremely limited scope for specialization and capitalistic production.

2. The Emergence of Indirect Exchange

Different goods have differing degrees of *marketability*. This is an attribute distinct from a good's value. For example, an oil well is more valuable (to most people) than a gold coin, but it is not nearly as marketable.

The possibility of indirect exchange gives individuals much more flexibility. Someone who wishes to trade eggs for shoes doesn't need to find a corresponding person who wishes to trade shoes for eggs (which would be the case in direct exchange). Rather, the egg seller has the option of achieving his desired goal *indirectly*, by first trading the eggs for butter (say) and then finding someone who wishes to trade shoes for butter.

Even if a seller doesn't have an actual third party in mind, he or she will still find it advantageous to trade away goods of lower marketability in exchange for goods of higher marketability. This will put the seller in a much more advantageous position when he or she enters the market looking for sellers of whatever commodities the seller wishes to purchase for direct use.

Chapter 3: The Pattern of Indirect Exchange 31

Over time, goods that were initially more marketable (in a state of direct exchange) will become even more so. For example, wheat and butter would likely be more marketable (in barter) than telescopes, because virtually everyone would wish to purchase some quantities of wheat and butter, while the market for telescopes would be much narrower. But this means that even people who did not want wheat or butter for direct use would be likely to accept them as *media of exchange*, because they would know that it would be quite easy to trade away the very marketable wheat and butter for whatever goods they ultimately desired. Hence, the marketability of wheat and butter would be enhanced with the possibility of indirect exchange.

Eventually, a few (or one) commodities would outstrip all rivals and become *commonly accepted* media of exchange, i.e., *money*. Attributes that contribute to the suitability of a good for becoming money are its divisibility, durability, ease of transport, and convenient exchange value per unit. Historically, gold and silver have proved to be excellent money goods. (In contrast, one would need to deliver huge amounts of wheat in order to buy a house or car, and butter spoils very quickly. Hence these goods, though more marketable than telescopes, would not likely become money.)

3. Some Implications of the Emergence of Money

Money allows for specialization in the stages of production. Entrepreneurs can use money to hire workers and purchase natural resources and capital goods, and then sell the enhanced capital goods (for money) to an entrepreneur in a lower order of production. The money proceeds can then be used to buy consumption goods for the entrepreneur. Money also allows for economic calculation, because entrepreneurs can compare money expenditures with money receipts to determine if they are efficiently using scarce resources.

32   *Study Guide to Man, Economy, and State with Power and Market*

4. The Monetary Unit

As it emerges on a free market, the money commodity will be traded in terms of weight (ounces, pounds, grams, etc.). The specific unit of weight in which prices are quoted is a matter of convenience; platinum trades in terms of ounces, while iron in terms of tons. The actual *form* in which the money commodity is traded is also a matter of convenience. Gold in the form of bars may be used for expensive transactions, while gold coins are used for smaller purchases.

5. Money Income and Money Expenditures

For a specified interval of time, an individual can keep track of his total money income and money expenditures in order to record his *balance of payments*. An individual can "purchase" money by selling goods and services in exchange for money. Another way to acquire units of money is to directly produce them (as in mining for gold).

The stock of money that an individual possesses is his or her *cash balance*. Note that there is no such thing as money "in circulation"; at any given time, every unit of money is owned by someone. For a specified time interval, we can write the following equation:

Money Income =
Money Expenditures + Net Additions to Cash Balance

6. Producers' Expenditures

People can spend their money not only on consumer goods but also goods of higher orders. The *capitalists* are those who invest money in factors of production.

Chapter 3: The Pattern of Indirect Exchange   *33*

7. Maximizing Income and Allocating Resources

Other things equal, people will strive for the highest possible money incomes. But "other things" are not always equal. A person may work at a job for a lower money wage because he enjoys the hours, or an investor may settle for a lower rate of return because he is fond of the company in question.

As the cash balance increases, the marginal utility of money declines. On the other hand, as the amount of leisure decreases, its marginal utility rises. A worker will continue to supply additional units of labor for money, until the utility of the next unit of leisure is higher than the utility of the money that could be earned by working for an additional unit of time.

Entrepreneurs can reap a monetary gain by "buying cheap and selling dear." This behavior will tend to correct inefficient allocations of resources.

Every actor must allocate his money resources among consumption spending, investment expenditure, and additions to his cash balance. The next chapter will explore the actual determination of money prices.

Notable Contributions

• Carl Menger's explanation of the origins of money (and his critique of the State theory) was the most thorough and rigorous of its time.

• Rothbard's figures 30 and 31 (pp. 190–91) are very useful to visualize the pattern of indirect exchange.

• As Rothbard points out (pp. 193–94), modern mainstream economics tends to analyze the economy in terms of direct exchange, and then add on money as an afterthought. Indeed, under the assumptions of typical mathematical models, goods would not have differing degrees of marketability and there would be no need for money at all.

• Contrast figure 32 (p. 208) with the typical "circular flow" diagram of mainstream macro textbooks. Only Rothbard's figure can capture the idea of a structure of production.

Technical Matters

1. Rothbard uses the terms *barter* and *direct exchange* interchangeably (p. 187). However, some economists use the term *barter economy* to refer to any economy without money. Technically, then, if we had an economy with media of exchange but not a commonly accepted medium, these economists would call it a barter economy while Rothbard would not.

2. In the discussion above, we used the example of building a house to illustrate the immense drawbacks of direct exchange. However, even if all of the listed obstacles were overcome, it is not clear whether the situation would even then be an example of direct exchange. By hypothesis, such a builder would have traded his goods away to workers, lumber owners, etc., *with the intention of trading away the product of their surrendered goods to another party*, i.e., the future home buyer. Thus, our hypothetical builder would still be engaging in *indirect* exchange. Indeed, the emergence of indirect exchange is so natural that it is hard to even imagine an economy of purely direct exchange.

3. In discussing marketability (or "saleability"), Menger says that a marketable good is one that can be quickly sold at an "economic" price. This is an important point, because often people think that an "unmarketable" good is one that cannot be sold. But if the asking price is low enough, virtually *any* good can be sold. Even so, there is certainly a sense in which a telescope (say) is much less marketable than wheat: the person selling the telescope (in barter) can get a much

36   Study Guide to Man, Economy, and State with Power and Market

better price if he is willing to spend weeks looking for prospective buyers, whereas the seller of wheat will probably find his best offer within hours.

4. Although in general it is certainly true that a neoclassical model has no role for a medium of exchange (because of perfect foresight and limited types of goods), there have been a few attempts to model the process captured by Menger's verbal description. In particular, Kiyotaki and Wright ("On Money as a Medium of Exchange," *Journal of Political Economy* 97, no. 4 [August 1989]: 927–54) devise a model with goods of varying marketability and actually cite Menger's pioneering work.

5. On page 204, Rothbard writes that money income equals money expenditures plus net additions to the cash balance *minus* net subtractions from the cash balance. This is somewhat confusing, because normally the term *net* would mean that the different episodes of adding and subtracting to the cash balance had already been compiled into one total figure. This is why, in the summary above, we have dropped the last term from the equation.

Chapter 3: The Pattern of Indirect Exchange

Study Questions

1. Name two *different* problems with direct exchange. (pp. 187–88)

2. Explain the term *medium of exchange*. (p. 189)

3. Why are some goods more marketable than others? (p. 190)

4. In what sense is a telescope relatively unmarketable (i.e., difficult to sell)? Couldn't the owner lower its price until he found a buyer?

5. What does it mean to purchase money? (p. 194)

6. What is the price of money?

7. Rothbard says that the unit of money is a weight. How does this apply to the U.S. dollar? (p. 197)

8. Why does the marginal utility of money decline as its supply increases? (p. 218)

9. How does a person decide whether to work for himself or an employer? (pp. 221–22)

10. How does the owner of a durable good decide whether to rent or sell it? (pp. 225–27)

CHAPTER 4

PRICES AND CONSUMPTION

Chapter Summary

In a money economy, the money commodity is on one side of every transaction, and hence reduces the number of relevant prices. The direct exchange ratio between any two commodities can easily be computed from their respective money prices. The "price" or *purchasing power* of money is the array of goods and services for which a unit of money can be exchanged.

Individual supply and demand schedules in a money economy are determined by the same principles applicable to a barter economy. An individual's value scale contains units of the money commodity as well as all other commodities and services, and the individual will engage in market exchanges to achieve the bundle of goods (including units of the money commodity) that he or she believes will yield the greatest utility. There have been various attempts to gauge the total "surplus" that individuals enjoy from the existence of markets, but these procedures suffer from methodological errors. Individuals benefit from voluntary exchanges, but it is nonsensical to ask how *much* they benefit, because utility is not a cardinal magnitude.

The utility from *selling* a good for money is the value of the most highly ranked use to which the additional money can be devoted (whether to spend on consumption, invest, or add to the cash balance). The utility from *buying* a good with money is

40   Study Guide to Man, Economy, and State with Power and Market

the value of the most highly ranked end (consumption, production, or future sale) to which the good can be devoted.

Unlike the position of other goods, the economist must offer some explanation for the precise position of units of money on individuals' value scales. In short, the economist must explain, not only the relative prices of real goods, but also their absolute *nominal* (money) prices. For example, why aren't money prices double, or half, of what they in fact are?

To explain the current purchasing power of money (PPM), the economist relies on the current *anticipations* of the *future* PPM. That is, people right now give up other goods for units of money, because these people expect that these units of money will be exchangeable for other goods in the near future. The current anticipations of future PPM, in turn, are explained by people's memories of the prices of the immediate past, i.e., by the past PPM. Ultimately, then, today's PPM is largely influenced by yesterday's PPM, and yesterday's PPM was in turn influenced by the day *before* yesterday's PPM, and so on. We push this explanation back until the moment when there were no media of exchange, and (what is now) the money commodity was valued solely for its direct use in consumption and/or production. (This is Mises's famous *regression theorem* or *money regression*.)

Durable goods yield a flow of *services* over time. The price of a service is the *rental* or *hire* price of the good and is determined by the marginal productivity or marginal utility of the service. The outright purchase price of a durable good is its *capitalized value*, and tends to equal the (discounted) present value of its total expected flow of future services.

Chapter 4: Prices and Consumption   *41*

Chapter Outline

1. Money Prices

The great advantage of a monetary economy is that the same commodity (i.e., the money good) is on one side of (almost) every transaction. In a barter economy there is a separate price or exchange ratio for each pair of goods. A simple question such as, "What is the price of a TV?" would have no simple answer. The TV might exchange for 1,000 berries, or ½ of a cow, or 5 radios. Before answering the question about its price we would need to clarify, "In terms of which good?"

The introduction of the money good simplifies things greatly. Because virtually *every* transaction involves the money commodity on one side, any good's price is quoted as its exchange ratio with the money commodity. Thus there are only as many prices as there are different commodities. There is a tendency for *one price* to emerge on the market for each separate commodity.

The direct exchange ratio between any two goods can easily be calculated once their respective money prices are known. However, one must not fall into the common trap of abstracting away from the role of money in the real world. Acting humans in modern economies do *not* exchange real commodities directly against each other, but almost always act through the medium of exchange.

When talking about the "price" of money, we mean its *purchasing power*. It is thus the *entire array* of goods and services that can be exchanged for one unit of the money commodity. (Notice that in barter, the price of *every* good is ultimately an array of its exchange ratios with all other goods.)

42   *Study Guide to Man, Economy, and State with Power and Market*

2. Determination of Money Prices

Money prices are generated by the actions of individuals, and must ultimately be explained by reference to individual value scales. Each individual in the market ranks various units of each commodity, including the money commodity, on an ordinal scale of value. The individual's demand schedule for each good in terms of money prices is then determined in the exact same way as under barter (chapter 2), except that here one of the goods happens to be the universally accepted medium of exchange. (In later sections we will analyze the precise *position* of the money commodity on the value scale.) Because of diminishing marginal utility, an individual's demand curve cannot be upward sloping. The summation of each potential buyer's demand schedule gives the *market* demand schedule, i.e., the number of units demanded at each hypothetical money price for the good. The determination of the market supply schedule is also comparable to the barter analysis. The *equilibrium* (money) *price* is the (money) price at which quantity supplied equals quantity demanded.

3. Determination of Supply and Demand Schedules

To the extent that actors correctly forecast the future equilibrium price in a market, their supply and demand schedules will become more elastic, and will hence speed the movement toward equilibrium. For a *given* stock of a good, the supply curve will tend to be almost vertical, as there is little else the owners can do besides sell the existing units for money.

4. The Gains From Exchange

All participants to voluntary exchange benefit; each values what he or she receives more than what he or she gives up. However, the mainstream technique of calculating consumer

Chapter 4: Prices and Consumption 43

and producer "surplus" is entirely fallacious. In this approach, a consumer who would have been willing to pay up to, say, $10 for the first unit of a good, but only has to pay the market price of $5, is said to enjoy $5 of surplus on this first unit. The smaller surpluses on subsequent units are calculated and added together to reveal this consumer's total surplus. Yet this procedure assumes (a) that we can deduce information from individual's value scales that are not revealed in action, (b) that money is a stable measuring rod of subjective value, and (c) that it makes sense to add "units of utility" together. Other attempts at measuring psychic surpluses involve interpersonal utility comparisons, and thus involve yet another fallacy.

5. The Marginal Utility of Money

A. The Consumer

As with all goods, the consumer allocates additional units of money to the most highly ranked end that is yet unsatisfied. Units of the money commodity can be (a) used in direct consumption, (b) exchanged for other consumption goods, (c) invested in factors of production, and (d) added to the cash balance. At any given time, *all* units of money in the economy are held by someone; there is no such thing as money "in circulation."

Options (b) through (d) above present an apparent problem: The marginal utility of a unit of money depends largely on the marginal utility of the various goods (consumer or producer) for which it can be exchanged; i.e., the marginal utility of money depends on its anticipated *purchasing power*. But to explain the purchasing power of money, the subjectivist cites the marginal utility of money. That is, people voluntarily give up real goods and services in exchange for units of money, because they value the money more than what is given up. Taken together, these two explanations seem to involve a circular argument, by which the purchasing power of money is ultimately explained by the purchasing power of money. In the next section we resolve this conundrum.

B. The Money Regression

To explain the current purchasing power of money, we must explain why people *right now* sacrifice valuable goods and services in exchange for units of the money commodity. They do this because (of course) the marginal utility they receive from the additional money units exceeds the marginal utility from the goods and services sold. But *why* do these units of money offer utility? Disregarding direct consumption, individuals derive utility from holding money units because they *anticipate* the possibility of exchanging them for goods and services *in the future*. Thus, the current purchasing power of money (PPM) is influenced by individuals' expectations about the PPM in the (perhaps immediate) *future*. Note that this explanation, so far, does not involve a circular argument, because we have introduced the time element.

Yet what governs the expectations of the future PPM? Mises argued that it was the experience of money's purchasing power in the immediate *past*. This is not a strict relation; people do not automatically assume that the PPM tomorrow will be identical to yesterday's PPM. But when trying to estimate the amounts of various goods and services that a unit of money will fetch tomorrow, individuals must naturally rely on recent prices.

Now it seems that we have merely transformed the problem of circularity into one of infinite regress: We explain today's PPM by yesterday's PPM. But *yesterday's*

Chapter 4: Prices and Consumption   *45*

PPM must be explained by the PPM the day *before* yesterday, and so on.

The regress is not infinite, however. Mises argued that we can trace back the PPM until the moment when the money commodity first emerged as a medium of exchange. Before then, the community was in a state of direct exchange, and hence the purchasing power (exchange value) of (what is now) the money commodity could be explained in the normal way, by reference to its marginal utility in consumption or production.

C. Utility and Costs

The utility from *selling* a good for money is the value of the most highly ranked use to which the additional money can be devoted (whether to spend on consumption, invest, or add to the cash balance). The cost of selling a good is the value of the most highly ranked alternative end (whether consumption, production, or future sale) to which the good could have been devoted, had it not been sold.

The utility from *buying* a good with money is the value of the most highly ranked end (consumption, production, or future sale) to which the good can be devoted. The cost of buying a good with money is the value of the most highly ranked alternative use (expenditure on consumption, investment, or addition to cash balance) that the units of money can no longer satisfy.

Ex ante refers to anticipations before an action, while *ex post* refers to judgments after an action. Thus an actor always maximizes his *ex ante* psychic revenue, i.e., the actor always chooses the end that he *predicts* will deliver the highest psychic revenue. But actors may

46   *Study Guide to Man, Economy, and State with Power and Market*

make mistakes, and may decide *ex post* that they should have chosen differently.

D.   Planning and the Range of Choice

Individuals in a market economy form their own plans based (in part) on the expectations of actions by other individuals. There is no reason to suppose that "central planning" will yield a better or more orderly outcome. In fact, as *Man, Economy, and State* demonstrates, there are systematic tendencies for the decentralized market pricing system to coordinate individual plans.

6.   Interrelations Among the Prices of Consumers' Goods

Goods are related by their *substitutability* or *complementarity*, as summarized on page 286. The more substitutes for any given good, the greater the elasticity of its demand schedules will tend to be.

7.   The Prices of Durable Goods and Their Services

Durable goods (whether producer or consumer) yield a flow of services over time. The price of a service is the *rental* or *hire* price of the good; it is how much someone would pay to use the durable good for a given period of time. The rental or hire price is determined by the marginal productivity (if a producer good) or marginal utility (if a consumer good) of the service.

The outright purchase price of a durable good is its *capitalized value*, and tends to equal the (discounted) present value of its total expected flow of future services. Because of time preference, an actor will not evaluate a given unit of service in the distant future the same as a unit of service available today or tomorrow. The process of capitalization explains why finite

Chapter 4: Prices and Consumption	*47*

prices are paid for (virtually) infinitely durable goods, such as land.

8. Welfare Comparisons and the Ultimate Satisfactions of the Consumer

All of the praxeological truths of chapter 1 are still applicable in a money economy. Ultimately, what the economist labels a "consumer good" in the market place may in fact truly be a higher-order good for the consumer, because so-called consumer goods (such as cans of Pepsi) are really just *means* to more ultimate ends (such as satisfying thirst).

9. Some Fallacies Relating to Utility

Mainstream economists often derive an equilibrium condition in which the marginal utility of each good, divided by the price of the good, is equal for all goods. The argument is that the marginal penny must yield the same increment in utility, regardless of the good on which it is spent, because if this *weren't* the case, then the consumer could achieve a greater amount of total utility by rearranging his or her expenditures. The fallacy here is that utility is not a cardinal concept, and hence it makes no *sense* to perform arithmetical operations on the "marginal utility" of a given good.

APPENDIX A:
The Diminishing Marginal Utility of Money

Money is a commodity and hence is subject to the law of diminishing marginal utility: the greater the units of money one has, the lower its marginal utility. In the case of money, we must be careful to maintain the *ceteris paribus* assumptions. For example, prices may change between the time that the 100th and

48   *Study Guide to Man, Economy, and State with Power and Market*

101st units of money are acquired, and this will affect the individual's estimate of their respective marginal utilities.

APPENDIX B:
On Value

There are many uses of the word *value*. In modern Austrian economics, the term usually refers to the *subjective value* an individual places on a good. However, in the present chapter the *capital value* of a durable good was its *objective exchange value* on the market, i.e., how many units of money could be obtained by selling the durable good. Economics is primarily the study of how underlying subjective valuations give rise to objective exchange values in the form of market prices.

Chapter 4: Prices and Consumption

Notable Contributions

• Rothbard's devastating critique of measuring psychic surpluses (pp. 258–60) is still relevant.

• Mises was the first economist to fully incorporate money into the subjectivist, marginal utility approach that economics had developed for the case of barter. His regression theorem evaded the apparent problem of circularity that had stumped earlier theorists. Before Mises, economists used "micro" analysis to explain barter exchange ratios, and then superimposed money prices using a "macro" approach involving "the price level" and the total stock of money. (See Rothbard's footnote 19 on pp. 269–70.)

• Figure 38 (p. 274) depicts the temporal elements of gold prices, during a state of first direct exchange and then indirect exchange.

• Rothbard ingeniously deals with the famous example of Buridan's ass (p. 310), which was placed equidistant between two equally attractive oases and dies of thirst. Rather than illustrating the relevance of indifference, this example merely shows its silliness. Only an ass would be unable to choose in such a situation, because to stand still would really be "choosing" to die of thirst, and this is clearly an inferior option.

50   Study Guide to Man, Economy, and State with Power and Market

Technical Matters

1. A barter economy with n goods would in principle require $n(n-1)/2$ different prices, one for each pair of commodities. (A barter economy with 20 different goods, for example, would require 190 different prices.) In contrast, a money economy with n goods only requires n prices, and the (money) price of the money commodity itself is of course always 1.

2. Mainstream economists no longer believe that diminishing marginal utility necessarily implies the Law of Demand. (Their argument would lie beyond the scope of this text.) Austrians should therefore take care when making this point to mainstream peers.

3. On page 252, Rothbard's first reason for holding a good is "(a) the *anticipated later sale* of the same good for a higher money price." Note that this "speculative" demand must also include the desire to hold certain commodities as a store of wealth, e.g., someone who buys rubies or even shares of stock with the intention of selling them later on may not necessarily anticipate a higher future money price.

4. As Rothbard points out in footnote 21 (p. 273), the "crucial stopping point" in the regression argument is not the point at which the money commodity ceases to be a universal medium of exchange, but rather the earlier point at which the commodity ceases to be a medium of exchange *at all*.

Chapter 4: Prices and Consumption 51

5. The classical economists believed that the factors Land, Labor, and Capital earned the income of Rents, Wages, and Profits (Interest) respectively. The Austrian view is entirely different: *All* productive factors (including land, labor, and capital goods) earn rents, and *all* durable goods yield interest over time. Consider a piece of land that can be rented for $1,000 annually to sharecroppers. If the capitalized value of the land is $10,000, then these annual *rents* of $1,000 are, at the same time, an annual *interest return* of 10 percent on the invested capital funds. (This example is adapted from Irving Fisher.)

6. The neoclassical economist would respond to Rothbard's critique (pp. 304–05) by claiming that mainstream economics no longer *really* believes in cardinal utility. Rather, through the use of "representation theorems," the modern neoclassical feels that he or she can use cardinal utility functions as a convenient shortcut, while still believing in the ultimate ordinality of consumer preferences. It is good that the neoclassical at least recognizes that utility is ordinal, but most Austrians would deny that the representation theorems are a valid justification for the continued mainstream use of cardinal utility functions.

Study Questions

1. What is the significance of the fact that the "number of markets needed is immeasurably reduced" in a money economy? (pp. 233–35)

2. Why doesn't *every* good have a purchasing power that consists of an array, i.e., what is so special about the money commodity? (pp. 236–37)

3. What does it mean to "sell" money? To "buy" money?

4. Why do individuals hold cash balances? (pp. 264–65)

5. Why does Rothbard argue that buying more eggs will make the marginal utility of butter increase? (p. 266)

6. Are money prices a measuring rod of subjective value?

7. Why did economists before Mises find difficulty with a marginal utility explanation of money demand? (p. 268)

8. How does Mises's money regression apply to fiat money?

9. Can an individual really know the true cost of an action, even *ex post*? (p. 277)

Chapter 4: Prices and Consumption   *53*

10. Does the diminishing marginal utility of money prove that a progressive income tax would increase total social utility? (p. 302)

CHAPTER 5

PRODUCTION: THE STRUCTURE

Chapter Summary

The evenly rotating economy (ERE) is an important tool in Misesian economics. The ERE is a fictitious construct where the future is certain, a world where economic activities repeat themselves indefinitely.

The ERE is primarily used to distinguish *profit* from *interest*. Entrepreneurs earn pure profits when they judge future conditions better than their rivals, while they suffer losses if they exercise poor foresight. In an uncertain world, a man may anticipate that consumer demand for a new product will be higher than others expect, and he will buy the factors necessary to produce the good and reap a much higher payment when he sells the finished product to consumers. This phenomenon is impossible in the ERE, because everyone knows exactly how much each good will fetch from consumers in the future. However, because capitalists advance *present* money to the owners of factors in order to sell goods to consumers *in the future*, the capitalists still earn more money from consumers than they had to pay to all of the factor owners who contributed to the production of the good. This excess would appear as a "profit" to an accountant, but not to an economist. It merely represents the interest earned by the capitalists on their invested funds. In the ERE the rate of return (per unit time) will be equal in all lines of production.

56   Study Guide to Man, Economy, and State with Power and Market

The difficult problem of analyzing the payments to various factors of production is broken down into simpler cases. In this chapter, we assume that all factors are completely specific, i.e., are useful only in the production of one good. We then deal with the case of joint ownership of the product by the factor owners; that is, the owners of land and labor each contribute their efforts to the maturing product, and then get paid their portion when the consumer purchases the finished good. The primary lesson from this analysis is that capitalists earn no independent return; ultimately all revenue from the sale to a consumer can be traced back to the owners of the original factors.

We later relax this assumption and allow for capitalists to pay the owners of land and labor *up front* for their services, in exchange for relinquishing ownership over the maturing capital goods as they move through the production process. In this more realistic scenario, the capitalists do indeed retain a certain portion of the total revenue spent by consumers. However, this revenue is due to the fact that the capitalists paid the workers and landowners *before* their services yielded revenues from the consumers. It is the agio on present versus future goods (*not* exploitation or superior bargaining power) that explains the discounted payment to the original factor owners.

Cost is a subjective, ephemeral concept. The cost of an action is immediately borne by the actor, and is known only to him. The classical economists, as well as Alfred Marshall, were mistaken when they argued that prices are somehow influenced by the "costs of production." The causality is completely the reverse: It is not the case that diamonds are expensive because they are costly to produce. On the contrary, diamond mines are expensive because consumers place a high marginal utility on diamonds. If one man takes ten hours to produce a good that another man can make in five hours, the first man cannot expect to earn a high price in the market because of his higher "costs."

Chapter 5: Production: The Structure 57

Chapter Outline

1. Some Fundamental Principles of Action

A review of concepts discussed earlier.

2. The Evenly Rotating Economy

The evenly rotating economy (ERE) is a fictitious mental construction in which all economic activities repeat themselves in a perfectly predictable manner. The ERE is the final end state toward which the market would tend if all disturbing influences were held at bay.

There is no uncertainty in the ERE. The ERE allows the conceptual distinction between *profit* and *interest*: Because there is certainty, there can be no profits or losses in the ERE. However, there is still time preference, and hence interest.

3. The Structure of Production: A World of Specific Factors

This section analyzes a hypothetical world in which each good is produced by several completely *specific* factors; i.e., each factor of production is suited to produce only one good. There is thus no "economic problem" in deciding on the allocation of factors: Once consumers decide upon which goods they desire, it is a simple matter to employ the factors in the proper fashion.

It is clear that the total revenue obtained from consumers for a given good must be the total incomes paid to the factors used in its production. To analyze the distribution of this total income among the various complementary factors, Rothbard deals with two possible cases: joint ownership versus ownership by the capitalists (sections 4 and 6 below, respectively).

4. Joint Ownership of the Product by the Owners of the Factors

In this simple case, Rothbard assumes that the owners of the (completely specific) factors, which are used in the production of a given consumer good, maintain joint ownership of the goods-in-process as they "move down the pipeline" from the highest orders to the final consumer good. The main purpose of this analysis is to drive home the point that there can be *no* independent return to the owners of capital goods; all income received at the point of final sale (from the consumer) ultimately flows to the owners of the original factors, land and labor.

5. Cost

The marginal cost of an action is the value placed on the next-best alternative. This is clearly a subjective concept, since value is subjective. No outside observer can determine the cost of someone's decision. Moreover, cost is "ephemeral" in the sense that, once a man acts, the best alternative course is *immediately* rendered unattainable. (If it were not, then its value would not really be a cost of the original action. One cannot *undo* an action, he can at best perform another action.) Because action is forward-looking, the costs of production have no bearing on the sale price of a good.

Notice that in the special case of completely specific factors, there is no cost to production. If a factor is suitable for the production of only one type of good, then its use for this end entails no foregone alternative. Where this is obviously not the case—such as a wooded area being inherently beautiful if not used for erecting a shopping mall, or labor hours being used for leisure if not devoted to a productive end—simply proves that in the real world, factors of production are not completely specific; they must be allocated among competing ends.

Chapter 5: Production: The Structure   *59*

6. Ownership of the Product by Capitalists: Amalgamated Stages

In this section Rothbard makes the more realistic assumption that, rather than the owners of land and labor waiting for their joint product to "ripen" into a final consumer good before receiving any income, instead the capitalists pay the owners of original factors at each stage of production. It is then the capitalists who retain ownership of the goods-in-process as they move down the pipeline from the highest order to the final consumer good. If there are no entrepreneurial errors, the capitalists will always receive more from the consumer than the sum total in payments made to the original factor owners.

This apparent change (from section 4, where the factor owners maintained joint ownership of the maturing product) is *not* due to "exploitation," and it does *not* indicate a separate return to the capitalists as such. In section 4, the factor owners had to wait until the final sale to the consumer before receiving any payment. For example, laborers in coal mines would have to wait years before receiving any income from their efforts. But the capitalists offer to pay workers (and land owners) *immediately* for services that will not yield finished consumer goods until the future. Thus, the capitalists are exchanging a present good (money) for a future good (the marginal product, in terms of the final consumer good, of the factor in question). The excess of the capitalists' income from consumers, over the sum of payments they make to the owners of original factors, is due to interest (i.e., time preference), and *not* to any bargaining power or other "contribution" of the capitalists.

7. Present and Future Goods: The Pure Rate of Interest

In the ERE there are no pure profits or losses. (Profits accrue to those who anticipate future conditions better than

60   *Study Guide to Man, Economy, and State with Power and Market*

other actors, but in the ERE there is no uncertainty.) However, present goods still exchange at a premium against future goods, and thus capitalists can still earn interest. In the ERE, the rate of return in all lines must be equal; if capitalists earned 5 percent in one line and 3 percent in another, then they would shift out of the latter and into the former until the rates were equal. The precise determination of the interest rate will be discussed in the following chapter.

The classical economists (as well as today's layman) thought that labor earned wages, land earned rent, and capital earned interest. This tripartite division is completely fallacious. All productive factors earn a (gross) rent or "hire price" per unit time in accordance with their marginal productivity, whether the factor is labor, a piece of land, or a machine.

8. Money Costs, Prices, and Alfred Marshall

The classical economists tended to think that prices were determined by the "costs of production" (at least in the long-run and for reproducible goods). After the marginal (or subjective) revolution in the 1870s, many economists (including the Austrians) stressed the primacy of utility in the determination of price. Alfred Marshall famously argued that cost (supply) and utility (demand) determined price together, and that to ask which cause dominated would be akin to asking which blade of a scissors did the cutting. The Austrian response to Marshall is that even supply curves are ultimately determined by marginal utility. There is no "real cost" (in an objective, technological sense) to anything; all actions, including decisions to produce, are accompanied by a marginal cost that itself flows from a subjective valuation.

It is true that in the ERE, money prices for consumer goods tend to equal money prices for factor payments (due account being made for interest). But this does not mean that money

Chapter 5: Production: The Structure 61

costs determine money prices. The consumer of a good does not care how much money a producer spent in its production; the price of a good is determined by its marginal utility to the consumer. If the utility of a certain consumer good is so low that a producer cannot afford to purchase the factors necessary for its construction, the producer will hire fewer of the factors and produce less of the good. This will tend to lower the rents (i.e., prices) earned by the factors, and the reduced supply of the good will raise its marginal utility to consumers. The process will continue until the sum total of factor payments (including interest) equals the sale price of the consumer good. This process explains the tendency that "price equals cost."

9. Pricing and the Theory of Bargaining

Because the analysis to this point has assumed completely specific factors of production, economics can say very little about the *distribution* of the income earned at each stage among the complementary factor owners. (We do know that the total income earned in a given stage must be discounted at the prevailing rate of interest.) Any voluntary agreement among the factor owners will leave them all better than if they did not produce at all, but we cannot predict what the actual agreement will be because of "zones of indeterminacy."

At the very end of the section Rothbard explicitly introduces the assumption that labor is scarcer than land. There are always uses to which labor may be devoted to increase human happiness—if only to be consumed as leisure by the laborer himself. In contrast, at any given time there are always "submarginal" plots of land and other natural resources. It simply does not pay to incorporate them into a production process. Note that this assumption is not an *a priori* truth, but an empirical observation.

Notable Contributions

• Mises's notion of the "evenly rotating economy" is his own invention. Other economists dealt with a stationary state, but Mises uses the concept to clarify the difference between profit and interest. This focus on the relationship between uncertainty and profit is not unique to the Austrians (e.g., Frank Knight), but Mises's attention to the merits and dangers of unrealistic constructions is quite rare.

• As mentioned in chapter 1, the "structure of production" approach is fairly unique to the Austrians. It clarifies and underscores the role of time in production.

• The Böhm-Bawerkian insight that capital goods earn no net return is an Austrian doctrine that most mainstream economists consider archaic. (Paul Samuelson ridiculed Joseph Schumpeter in this regard.) But it is a completely logical extension of the ERE analysis.

• Rothbard's piecemeal approach to the problem of factor payments—first assuming completely specific factors and joint ownership, then relaxing the assumption of joint ownership, and finally (in a later chapter) relaxing the assumption of complete specificity—is an extremely helpful innovation that is not present in *Human Action*. Moreover, his diagram illustrating the factor payments at various stages is another pedagogical device that clarifies the analysis of the ERE.

Chapter 5: Production: The Structure 63

• The Austrian position on the utility-versus-real-costs controversy, and on Alfred Marshall's famous eclecticism, is quintessentially subjectivist. Austrians since Carl Menger have viewed market phenomena as the expression of underlying human valuations. The objective facts of technological recipes, resource supplies, and so forth are merely the means through which these valuations are expressed.

64   Study Guide to Man, Economy, and State with Power and Market

Technical Matters

1. In mainstream economics, a state of equilibrium means merely that there are no pure profit opportunities. Moreover, mainstream theorists will often use a construction involving perfect foresight *and* changing conditions. (For example, the seasons might vary, requiring the production of parkas in the winter but bathing suits in the summer. Yet so long as all of these fluctuations are perfectly anticipated, the prices of all factors will reflect their [discounted] marginal productivity.) Mises's construction of the ERE does not readily handle this type of situation, and care must be taken in generalizing results that are true in the ERE but not necessarily so in a world of perfectly predictable change. In particular, the ERE is a special case of the general equilibrium construct along the lines of Arrow-Debreu.

2. Note that the ERE does not in fact require complete recurrence of all events. For example, Mises notes in *Human Action* that people can still die, and new babies can still be born, in the ERE, so long as the effects are offsetting and do not influence the quantities of goods and services demanded by consumers.

3. There are some subtle complications in Rothbard's discussion of bargaining theory (section 9). In the first place, it makes a great difference if each of the completely specific factors is also *indispensable* for the production of its respective good. If this is not the case, then marginal principles can still be brought to bear in the pricing problem, even when each factor is completely specific. The factor owner would then be

Chapter 5: Production: The Structure
65

incapable of commanding more than the market value of that portion of the final product that would be diminished were he to withhold his inputs. (For example, suppose Smith and Jones own parcels of land of equal size that are only useful for the production of a certain type of berry. If Smith's land is twice as fertile as Jones's, then Smith will necessarily earn a higher income than Jones. Of course, Rothbard could deal with this case by designating one type of good "berries produced by Smith" and another "berries produced by Jones.") On the other hand, when each factor is not only completely specific, but also indispensable for the final good (and this seems to be what Rothbard has in mind), then marginal principles are not helpful at all, because the "marginal product" of each factor is apparently the entire finished product. (For example, marginal principles are not helpful in evaluating the relative importance of various ingredients in a cake. If we take away the eggs, we will not simply have less cake, we will not really have a cake at all.)

66   *Study Guide to Man, Economy, and State with Power and Market*

Study Questions

1. How does Rothbard justify study of the ERE, when Austrians are so critical of unrealistic assumptions in mainstream economics? (pp. 322–23)

2. Why is the ERE not only unrealistic, but indeed self-contradictory? (pp. 328–29)

3. How would Rothbard classify those goods that produce second-order capital goods? (pp. 330–31)

4. Describe the structure of production in a world of purely specific factors. (pp. 330–31)

5. In the case of joint ownership, where the final product is a diamond ring, arrange the following in order of their respective waiting times to be paid: (a) the truck driver bringing diamonds to the jeweler, (b) the laborer in the diamond mine, and (c) the jeweler who sets the diamond on a ring. (pp. 334–37)

6. What is wrong with the "freedom-to-starve" argument? (p. 339)

7. How can a sale be costless? (p. 341)

8. What is the problem with so-called "cost-plus" pricing schemes for public utilities (in which the

Chapter 5: Production: The Structure 67

utility companies are allowed to charge consumers what their "costs" are plus a certain percentage markup)? (pp. 341–42)

9. By what process does one pure rate of interest
    arise in the ERE? (p. 351)

10. Can a landowner earn interest in the ERE? (pp.
    351–53)

CHAPTER 6

PRODUCTION: THE RATE OF INTEREST AND ITS DETERMINATION

Chapter Summary

In the evenly rotating economy (ERE), capitalists must earn the same rate of return per time period, regardless of the good or the stage in which they invest. (Outside the ERE, arbitrage brings about a tendency for this result.)

Individuals can place various units of future goods on their value scales, along with various units of present goods. For example, an individual might prefer two units of steak next year over one unit of steak this year. (Because of time preference, an individual will always prefer the *same* quantity of a given good earlier rather than later.) A different individual, however, might consider one unit of present steak to give more utility than two units of future steak. There is thus a potential gain from trade, with the first individual selling one unit of present steak in exchange for the other individual's promise to deliver two units of steak next year. The *pure rate of interest* (i.e., exchange rate between present and future goods) will be established by the various individuals' time preferences in the same way that any other price is established.

The pure rate of interest manifests in every aspect of the "time market," whether this is the formal market for loans (with the rate of interest explicitly set by contract), or in the market for producer goods, where the rate of interest is implicit in the

69

price spread between a collection of inputs and their future output.

The role of the capitalists is to provide an "advance" to factor owners in exchange for the future consumer goods that these factors help yield. Because present goods exchange for future goods at a premium, the capitalist who invests in a particular process ends up with more capital funds than he started with. This "excess" return is not due to the productivity of the inputs, but instead to the fact that present goods are subjectively preferred to future goods. (Although land and labor owners sell future goods in exchange for present goods, this is only necessarily true in their "pre-income" state. After they have been paid for their original factor services, they may invest the proceeds in future goods themselves.)

The mainstream view of the ERE is very misleading. By focusing on "value added" at each stage, the mainstream theorist overlooks the importance of *gross investment* by the capitalists. This leads to a faulty emphasis on consumer spending as the barometer of an economy's health, when in fact this is relatively unimportant and will take care of itself. *Production* is the real challenge. Once the appropriate goods are produced, it is not difficult to coax people into consuming them.

The mainstream explanation of the determination of the rate of interest is also superficial. The "eclectic" theorist posits an interaction between subjective time preferences and objective rates of return. However, these rates of return are merely the price spreads in various stages of production, and themselves can only be explained by time preference.

There are many forces that affect an individual's rate of time preference, other things equal. For example, as his supply of present goods falls, his time preference increases.

Chapter 6: Production: The Rate of Interest and Its Determination 71

Chapter Outline

1. Many Stages: The Pure Rate of Interest

Up to this point, our analysis has assumed complete vertical integration, in which capitalists buy all of the factors of production and wait until the final consumer good is sold before recouping their investment. But in the real world, the production of a good is broken up into many stages, where different capitalists buy factors and capital goods from a higher stage, and then sell the resulting processed capital good to someone else at a lower stage in the process. In this case, the capitalists must actually receive interest income at these intermediate points (and not merely earn the appropriate overall rate of interest at the end of the process, given its total duration).

In the evenly rotating economy (ERE), there is no uncertainty and hence no pure profits. However, there is time preference, and a corresponding discount on future goods. Thus capitalists still earn interest income in the ERE. The rate of return (per unit of time) on capital investments must not only be equal for each good (as established earlier), but it must also be equal for every stage of each good. (If the rate of return were higher in a given stage, then capitalists would switch into it, bidding up the prices of the inputs and pushing down the price of its output. This would continue until the rate of return were equal to that of the other stages.) These facts are all summarized in Figure 41 (p. 369).

In the Austrian view, the role of the capitalists is to provide an "advance" to factor owners in exchange for the future consumer goods that these factors help yield. For example, a hired hand who fertilizes a field wants to be paid now so that he can buy his dinner, even though his labor will not actually produce food until several months have passed. Because present goods exchange for future goods at a premium, the capitalist who invests in this process ends up with more capital funds than he started with. This "excess" return is not due to the productivity of the farmland, or of the capital goods such as tractors used on the farm, but instead is due to the fact that present goods are subjectively preferred to future goods.

2. The Determination of the Pure Rate of Interest: The Time Market

The *pure rate of interest* is the premium on present goods that exists in the ERE. That is, it is the ratio of the price of present goods to present claims on those same goods to be delivered in the future. For example, if the pure rate of interest is 5 percent per annum, then in the ERE 100 gold ounces today will exchange for 105 ounces delivered in one year. This pure rate of interest will manifest itself in all "time markets," including not only the loan market but also markets for the factors of production. The pure rate of interest is ultimately determined by subjective time preferences.

3. Time Preference and Individual Value Scales

An individual can rank prospective and currently held *future* goods on his or her value scale, just as he or she can rank any goods in the current time period. Thus, an individual might prefer two units of steak next year over one unit of steak this year. (Because of time preference, an individual will always prefer the *same* quantity of a given good earlier rather than later.) A different individual, however, might consider one unit of present steak to give more utility than two units of future steak. There is thus a potential gain from (intertemporal) trade, with the first individual selling one unit of present steak in exchange for the other individual's promise to deliver two units of steak next year. The pure rate of interest (i.e., exchange rate between present and future goods) will be established by the various

Chapter 6: Production: The Rate of Interest and Its Determination 73

individuals' time preferences in the same way that any other price is established. The *demand* for present goods is constituted by the *supply* of future goods, and vice versa. Although we cannot compare the marginal utility that various individuals enjoy from present and future goods, we can certainly compare their time preference schedules.

4. The Time Market and the Production Structure

Although we can isolate the net return to capitalists—which, we recall, is due to the delay between the time of investment and turning over the resulting product to either a capitalist in a lower stage or to the final consumer—it is important to remember that the capitalists must decide every period to repeat their *gross investments* if a given production process is to be maintained. (The typical treatment in mainstream macro, especially its warnings about "double counting" in calculating GDP, tends to consider only *net* investment.) Production processes do not continue automatically; the capitalist at each stage of a process has the ability to drop out and spend all of his or her revenues (from last period's sale) on consumption. The mainstream emphasis (in both academia and the media) on the importance of consumer spending is totally unwarranted. It is ultimately the *price spreads* (i.e., the difference between the prices of inputs and the price of corresponding output) and their relation to the prevailing rate of time preference that determine the profitability of a given operation. The absolute amount of money that consumers are willing to spend on a given product is, by itself, completely irrelevant.

5. Time Preference, Capitalists, and Individual Money Stock

An individual's marginal rate of time preference will depend on his or her cash balance (both in the present and the expected

74   *Study Guide to Man, Economy, and State with Power and Market*

cash balance in the future). For example, as an individual enters the time market by selling present goods in exchange for (a greater number of) future goods, the marginal utility of present goods rises while the marginal utility of future goods falls. At some point the individual will refrain from selling an additional unit of present goods, no matter how high the rate of interest.

6. The Post-Income Demanders

We may analyze the time market decisions of individuals in their pre- and post-income states. For example, a landowner necessarily sells future goods in exchange for present goods when he rents his field to a sharecropper in exchange for gold ounces. However, after receiving this income, the landowner may then enter the time market and use his gold ounces to buy a bond from a corporation.

7. The Myth of the Importance of the Producers' Loan Market

The typical mainstream view of interest claims to be "eclectic" as opposed to the allegedly dogmatic or one-sided Austrian emphasis on time preference alone. The mainstream view is that the equilibrium rate of interest is determined by the interaction of both subjective time preference and objective "investment opportunities." This approach is epitomized in the diagram of the loanable funds market (p. 421), where the supply curve is admittedly determined by time preferences of lenders, but where the demand curve is allegedly determined by the rates of return on various projects. Thus, at a rate of interest of 5 percent, a businessperson will borrow funds to invest only in those projects that yield at least a 5 percent return (revenues over expenditures), while at a lower interest rate the businessperson would borrow a greater quantity of funds because now *more* projects are profitable. The fallacy here is that the

Chapter 6: Production: The Rate of Interest and Its Determination   75

supposedly "given" rates of return on various projects are nothing but the *price spreads* in those particular stages of production, and are themselves ultimately determined by time preference. If it were not for time preference, why wouldn't the prices of inputs for some given project be bid up to the expected future revenue (and hence lead to a zero rate of return)? Indeed, we can imagine an economy with no formal "producers' loan market" at all, where capitalists directly invest in inputs without resort to a financial intermediary. Hence the pure rate of interest has nothing essentially to do with the producers' loan market.

8. The Joint-Stock Company

Various individuals may pool their capital and exercise *joint ownership* over the assets and liabilities of a company. There are various methods of exercising control over such an entity; one popular method is to allow each shareholder one vote per share of stock.

9. Joint-Stock Companies and the Producers' Loan Market

In the ERE, there is no essential difference between a corporation's shareholders and its creditors; both groups "own" portions of the corporation. In the ERE, the *contractual* rate of interest will equal the *natural* rate of interest. In other words, the formal premium granted to lenders will be the same premium implicit in the price spreads in factor markets. However, if a particular line of production is unusually odious or revered, the rate of return may be lower or higher than the prevailing contractual rate. For example, if most investors believe cigarettes are a disgusting product, then they may require a higher rate of return to invest in this line than they require to invest their funds in the production of teddy bears. (This distaste must be very widespread to have such an effect.)

10. Forces Affecting Time Preference

Although praxeology cannot explain ultimate value judgments, it can make *ceteris paribus* statements regarding preferences. The higher a person's real income in the present, the lower will be his time preference. If the world were expected to end in one week, on the other hand, everyone's time preferences would rise incredibly.

11. The Time Structure of Interest Rates

Although mainstream writers often contrast the long rate of interest with the short, and construct the equilibrium long rate of interest as a function of the expected short rates, this approach fails to explain why there should be any divergence in the first place. As we have already seen, in the ERE the rate of return must be the same for a given duration of the investment.

APPENDIX:
Schumpeter and the Zero Rate of Interest

Joseph Schumpeter reached the famous (and controversial) conclusion that in long-run equilibrium, the rate of interest would be zero, since the prices of products would be imputed back to the prices of their inputs. Only with technological development could a positive interest rate be maintained. The Austrians, in contrast, stress that even in the "stationary," certain world of the ERE, there will always be time preference, and hence there will always exist a price spread between inputs and their outputs, i.e., the natural rate of interest will still be positive.

Notable Contributions

• Rothbard's figure 41 (p. 369) is perhaps the most economical depiction of the Austrian approach to capital and interest. Like the mainstream "circular flow diagram," figure 41 shows how, in the ERE, total expenditures (100 ounces of gold) equal total income (17 ounces to capitalists and 83 ounces to land and labor owners). However, figure 41 goes far beyond the typical macro diagram by depicting the structure of production, i.e., the fact that goods take *time* to mature from original factors into final consumer goods.

• Rothbard's critique (p. 401) of the concept of *gross national product* is relevant even today.

78 *Study Guide to Man, Economy, and State with Power and Market*

Technical Matters

1. At several places in this chapter, Rothbard states that a multi-year rate of interest (in the ERE) must equal the appropriate multiple of the annual rate. For example, "A production process or investment covering a period of two years will, in equilibrium, then earn 10 percent, the equivalent of 5 percent *per year*" (p. 372). This simplification is common in economics (especially when the number of years is low), but strictly speaking the appropriate two-year rate of interest would need to be 10.25 percent, because of compounding.

2. Note that in Rothbard's discussion on pp. 380–84, he is assuming that the future ounces of gold will be delivered in ten years. That is why he says that a market rate of interest of 2 percent (not 20 percent!) implies that "12 future ounces would be the price of 10 present ounces" (p. 381). As noted in the point above, Rothbard is here ignoring compound interest, and simply assumes that 2 percent per year for ten years translates into a 20 percent increase overall.

3. Rothbard's numerical choices illustrate an interesting possibility, that an individual might be neither a lender nor a borrower (p. 384). This may surprise the reader, who may have been thinking along the lines of, "If the interest rate is higher than an individual's initial time preference rate, he will lend, while if it is lower, he will borrow." This quick reasoning is not entirely valid, because of the difference in marginal utility of the $(N+1)$th unit versus the $(N-1)$th unit.

Chapter 6: Production: The Rate of Interest and Its Determination   79

4. Although his discussion is cogent (pp. 440–41), Rothbard fails to explain why there would even be investment trusts in the ERE. If there is no uncertainty, why would anyone pay others a fee for investing his money?

5. Rothbard's critique (pp. 446–49) of Lutz's theory of the interest rate structure is perfectly valid in the ERE. However, many mainstream theorists would argue that outside of the ERE, it is perfectly reasonable that the annualized rate of return on, say, a ten-year bond would be more than the corresponding yields of one-year bonds rolled over ten times. This is because the ten-year bond "locks in" the investment, and hence has less *liquidity* than the successive investment in one-year bonds. (Of course, the ability to sell bonds before maturity mitigates this contrast.)

6. When Schumpeter's disciples dismissed "time preference," they were not merely assuming their conclusion as Rothbard suggests (p. 451). For these theorists, *time preference* is defined as the subjective discount on future utility, and it is neither necessary nor sufficient for a discount on future *goods*. For example, a person might have no time preference in Clemence and Doody's sense, but might still prefer a present apple to a future apple (perhaps because his expected supply of future apples will be much higher than his current supply). This approach ultimately rests on a cardinal conception of utility (where time preference may be explicitly defined as the premium on a present *util*) and is, naturally, inconsistent with the Austrian view.

Study Questions

1. How is the analysis in this chapter more general than in the preceding chapters? (pp. 367–68)

2. Why is there a tendency for a uniform rate of interest? (pp. 370–71)

3. What is the "classical trinity"? (p. 373)

4. In what sense do laborers sell future goods and buy present goods? (p. 373–74)

5. Is it a violation of subjectivism to compare time preference schedules between individuals? (p. 385)

6. What is Rothbard's critique of "gross national product"? (p. 401)

7. What are the components of the time market? (pp. 417–18)

8. What is the par value of a stock? (p. 430)

9. Is there an important distinction between dividends and "retained earnings"? (p. 440)

10. If everyone's time preference is subjective, how can we speak of "the" natural rate of interest? Won't it be different for different people?

CHAPTER 7

PRODUCTION: GENERAL PRICING
OF THE FACTORS

Chapter Summary

This chapter explains the determination of prices for *unit factor services* in the ERE. A capitalist will be willing to hire an additional unit of a productive resource so long as its rental price is lower than its *discounted marginal value product* (DMVP). The marginal value product (MVP) is the additional revenue that can be imputed to the marginal unit of a productive factor. The discounted MVP is then simply the *present market value* of the (future) MVP. For example, if an additional hour of labor will generate $110 of additional revenue in one year's time, a prospective employer will pay no more than $100 *today* to hire this worker if the interest rate is 10 percent.

Although many authors stress the importance of variability in the proportion of inputs, it is actually the relative *specificity* of factors that allows a unique determination of DMVP.

The MVP is determined by the marginal physical product (MPP) times the price of the product. That is, the prospective buyer estimates the increased physical output (i.e., quantity of the good to be sold) due to an additional unit of a factor, and multiplies this by the market price of these extra goods. (To the extent that the market price of the final product declines as additional units are produced, the true MVP will actually be less than this computation would suggest.)

81

Although *land* is usually defined as the original, nature-given factors, while *capital goods* are usually defined as "produced means of production," these are not the ideal definitions. It is better to classify any productive factor that is *reproducible* as a capital good, and all other factors as either land or labor. In particular, depletable natural resources such as oil and coal should be classified as land, even though they are nonpermanent. Note that an actual piece of geographic land may consist of both economic land and capital goods, to the extent that maintenance must be performed (to combat erosion, etc.). In the ERE we cannot deal with depletable resources, since stocks of goods are not allowed to change over time.

Because all productive assets possess a capitalized value (which is equal to the present discounted value of all future rental payments in the ERE), in a sense the only incomes in the ERE are labor and interest on invested financial capital. For example, even someone who discovers an unowned plot of land that yields $10,000 in annual rents, is still (in the ERE) merely earning an implicit interest return on his capital "investment." This is because the market value of his land will be $200,000 (assuming a 5 percent rate of interest), and thus if the man chooses to receive the annual rental payments, he is forgoing the potential $200,000 in present goods.

Chapter 7: Production: General Pricing of the Factors   *83*

Chapter Outline

1. Imputation of the Discounted Marginal Value Product

In this chapter we will explore the pricing of *unit services* as they would be in the evenly rotating economy (ERE), and hence as they *tend* to be in the real world.

A capitalist will be willing to hire an additional unit of a productive resource so long as its rental price is lower than its *discounted marginal value product* (DMVP). The marginal value product (MVP) is the additional revenue that can be imputed to the marginal unit of a productive factor. The *discounted* MVP is then simply the *present market value* of the (future) MVP. For example, if an additional hour of labor will generate $110 of additional revenue in one year's time, a prospective employer will pay no more than $100 *today* to hire this worker if the interest rate is 10 percent.

Additional units of supply are allocated to uses that are less and less urgent. Consequently, the MVP (and DMVP) of a factor declines as its supply increases.

A *nonspecific* factor (i.e., one used in several lines of production) will be priced according to DMVP, where each successive unit is assigned to the most productive, yet unfulfilled, use. A *specific* factor's DMVP is calculated as the difference between the unit price of the final product and the sum of the prices of the nonspecific factors used in its production. For example, the nonspecific factor of labor may have a DMVP of $10 per hour. If one dose of a certain medicine can be created with one hour of labor and one pound of a certain type of berry, and this berry has no other economic use, then the DMVP of the pound of berries will be equal to the (discounted) price of the dose of medicine (as determined by marginal utility to consumers) minus the $10 payment to the worker.

2. Determination of the Discounted Marginal Value Product

A. Discounting

If a prospective purchaser or employer knows what the marginal value product of a factor will be, he or she simply discounts this future sum by the prevailing market rate of interest in order to determine the *discounted* marginal value product. For example, if one hour of labor *now* will yield additional consumer goods that will fetch an additional $105 of revenue *next year*, then the present market value of this labor (and hence its price in the ERE) will only be $100 if the interest rate is 5 percent.

B. The Marginal Physical Product

The marginal physical product (MPP) of a unit factor service is simply the *additional* units of goods that it yields. For example, the MPP of the tenth textile worker might be 50 shirts, because (say) nine workers produce 700 shirts, while ten workers produce 750 shirts. The average physical product (APP), in contrast, is the total quantity of product divided by the total units of the factor. In our example, the APP would be 75 shirts (750 shirts divided by 10 workers).

The law of returns implies that the APP curve will reach a maximum; i.e., at some point, further units of the factor will *lower* APP. In ranges of the quantity of factor where MPP is higher than APP, APP tends to rise. In ranges where MPP is lower than APP, APP falls. (Consider a student who has test scores of 80, 80, 90, and 90. If the student's fifth test is *higher* than his current average of 85, it will pull up his *new* average. If the student's fifth test score is *lower* than his current average, then his new

Chapter 7: Production: General Pricing of the Factors 85

average will be lower than 85.) Because of these facts, APP is maximized at that quantity of factor where MPP equals APP.

C. Marginal Value Product

Once the MPP is known, the MVP is determined by multiplying the MPP by the market price of the final good. To continue with the example from above, if shirts sell for $20 each, then the MVP of the tenth worker is $20 x 50 shirts = $1,000. (However, note the caveats in appendix A.)

3. The Source of Factor Incomes

What is the source of income—capital or consumption? In one sense, the goal of all capitalistic production is consumption. Furthermore, all producers are ultimately guided by the spending decisions of final consumers. However, except for direct processes (such as picking berries), production requires prior savings. In particular, workers demand payment *now* even though their efforts will only yield consumer goods in the future. Only the capitalists, who have accumulated the "wages fund" (to use the classical terminology), can allow the workers to be paid in advance for their product.

4. Land and Capital Goods

Although the conventional definition of capital goods is that they are "produced means of production," it is better to define them as *reproducible* means of production. Recall that the primary analytical purpose for the distinction between capital and land is that, in the ERE, capital goods earn no *net* return, precisely because they can be (re)produced with land and labor factors.

Geographic land is actually a combination of land (in the economic sense) and capital goods. For example, farms require deliberate maintenance to combat erosion, etc.

5. Capitalization and Rent

The market price or *capitalized value* of a durable asset will, in the ERE, be equal to the sum of its future rental earnings (due to the asset's flow of services), discounted appropriately by the rate of interest. In one sense, only laborers earn "pure rent" in the ERE, and the only types of income are wages and interest. This is true because even land factors have a capitalized value, and hence the rental payments accruing to their owners are (if only implicitly) interest returns due to time preference. For example, even someone who discovers an unowned plot of land that yields $10,000 in annual rents, is still (in the ERE) merely earning an implicit interest return on his capital "investment." This is because the market value of his land will be $200,000 (assuming a 5 percent rate of interest), and thus if the man chooses to receive the annual rental payments, he is forgoing the potential $200,000 in present goods.

6. The Depletion of Natural Resources

As we have seen, permanent, nonreproducible factors are classified as *land*, while goods that can wear out but are reproducible are classified as *capital goods*. But what of nonpermanent, nonreproducible productive resources, such as diamond mines? The crucial test is whether such resources can be reproduced by land and labor factors, and the answer is no. Hence depletable resources (oil, natural gas, etc.) are to be classified as land. (Note that we cannot deal with such resources in the ERE, since by definition stocks of resources cannot change over time.)

Chapter 7: Production: General Pricing of the Factors   87

APPENDIX A:
Marginal Physical and Marginal Value Product

Strictly speaking, it is not true that MVP equals MPP times price. This is because, as the quantity of goods increases, the Law of Demand requires that the price consumers will pay for them declines. In general, then, MVP will be *less* than MPP times price. To continue with our example from above, suppose that nine workers produce 700 shirts, and that the firm can charge $21 per shirt if it wants consumers to purchase 700 of them. Suppose that hiring a tenth worker will allow a total of 750 shirts to be produced, but that the firm can only charge $20 per shirt if it wants consumers to purchase 750 of them. In this case, the total increase in revenue (from hiring the tenth worker) is only $300 (i.e., $15,000 − $14,700), and not $1,000. Thus the firm would only pay up to $300 to hire the tenth worker (ignoring discounting). In effect, the lower product price is causing the firm to "lose" $1 on the first 700 units, and this offsets the direct $1,000 in revenue attributable to the tenth worker's MPP.

APPENDIX B:
Professor Rolph and the Discounted Marginal Productivity Theory

Rolph, a follower of Knight, disputes the DMVP approach and instead insists that every productive factor receives its payment directly. For example, workers who begin construction on a factory are paid at the end of the day, in exchange for the "product" that they have produced during the day; there is no discounting involved. However, this begs the question as to why an unfinished factory commands any price at all. It is clearly only because a higher order producer anticipates revenues from lower order producers, who in turn expect to sell goods to final consumers. If the factory turns out to be worthless (perhaps because it is located on a major fault line and is destroyed by an earthquake), it will be clear that the workers really didn't "produce" anything valuable at all, and were paid on the basis of entrepreneurial error.

Chapter 7: Production: General Pricing of the Factors 89

Notable Contributions

• Rothbard (pp. 454–56) clarifies the importance of *specificity*, rather than fixed vs. variable proportions, in the determination of factor prices.

• Rothbard's treatment of the definition of *land* (pp. 483–84) is an important clarification. Earlier definitions relied on backward-looking measures and could not handle odd cases (such as lightning striking a tree limb and creating a perfect spear).

90   *Study Guide to Man, Economy, and State with Power and Market*

Technical Matters

1. The mainstream worry over "fixed proportions" (pp. 454–55) is due to the apparent difficulty of using a marginal productivity approach in these cases. As an analogy, how can we determine the relative importance of members of The Beatles? If you take away Paul McCartney, the quality of the music suffers tremendously, but if you take away Ringo, the same is true; without a drummer, even the other three members wouldn't sound very good. Yet this would lead us to conclude that the entire value of The Beatles's music is due to Ringo. (This apparent problem doesn't arise with *variable* proportions of inputs. For example, if 10 tractors and 5 workers yield $1,000 of crops, while 10 tractors and 4 workers yield $900 of crops, then the marginal value product of the fifth worker is obviously $100.)

2. Going along with the above note, Rothbard deals with such an example on pp. 459–60. The mainstream economist would probably object to Rothbard's conclusion that the MVP of one unit of X is 25 gold ounces. For by the same reasoning, Rothbard would have to conclude that the MVP of 2.5 Y, as well as the MVP of .5 Z, were *also* both equal to 25 gold ounces. There is thus a suspicion that the application of the marginal productivity approach leads to "double (or triple) counting." However, notice that Rothbard is *not* saying that the firm, initially starting in a position of owning $3X$, $7.5Y$, and $1.5Z$, would pay up to 25 gold ounces to acquire an additional unit of X. Rather, Rothbard is saying that the firm starting out with $4X$, $10Y$, and $2Z$ would be willing to pay up

Chapter 7: Production: General Pricing of the Factors   *91*

to 25 gold ounces to *retain* the fourth unit of X. Also, if Rothbard had included the decrease in expenditures that would be possible from buying fewer units of Y and Z (when the firm loses one unit of X), then the loss of gold would be mitigated and there would be no question of "double counting." So long as care is taken to correctly specify the actual circumstances facing the decision-maker, the marginal productivity approach gives the correct answer.

3. Although everything Rothbard says in appendix B is correct, the Austrian should remember that a typical employer might not view himself as paying a discounted MVP. If the structure of production is not vertically integrated, then each producer buys inputs and sells his output to the next producer in line. These lower order producers in effect are the "consumers," and it doesn't really matter to the seller of iron ore what eventually happens to it. But the fundamental point is that the prices of higher order goods are causally determined by the prices of lower order goods, not vice versa.

92   *Study Guide to Man, Economy, and State with Power and Market*

Study Questions

1. What is a production process characterized by *fixed proportions*? (pp. 454–55)

2. Why must a factor's MVP be discounted?

3. Give an example of a highly specific factor. (p. 456)

4. Why does DMVP diminish as the supply of a factor increases? (p. 461)

5. What is the difference between the "general" and "particular" DMVP schedules for a factor? (p. 464)

6. Why will a factor always be employed in a region of declining APP? (p. 474)

7. Why does the Knightian reject the distinction between land and capital goods? (p. 483)

8. Under what circumstances would a forest be classified as land, or as a capital good?

9. Is Rothbard saying that land earns no rents in the ERE? (p. 495)

10. If MVP is not actually equal to MPP times price, what *is* its precise definition? (pp. 501–03)

CHAPTER 8

PRODUCTION: ENTREPRENEURSHIP AND CHANGE

Chapter Summary

Entrepreneurial *profit* occurs when someone buys factors at a certain price and sells the resulting product for a certain price, such that he reaps a higher rate of return than the prevailing rate of interest. Such an entrepreneur has taken advantage of a general *undervaluation* of the particular factors; had others generally been aware of the future sale price of the product, they too would have entered into this market (to earn the higher rate of return). Entrepreneurial *loss* entails the opposite, in which a capitalist invests in relatively overvalued resources only to find that he can sell the product at a price that does not correspond to the rate of interest.

In the ERE such over- or undervaluations are impossible, because the future is known with certainty. Every factor will be paid its correct DMVP. In the real world, entrepreneurship establishes a *tendency* for correct factor prices.

Starting from an initial long-run equilibrium, we can imagine a fall in time preferences. Then people will spend less on present consumption and will devote more to investment. Gross investment will be higher this period than last period, meaning there is positive *net* investment. This change will free up factors that were previously employed in lower stages, and allow them to be directed into the higher stages. This "lengthening" of the production structure corresponds to a more "capitalistic"

93

process. The price spreads will fall between stages, corresponding to a lower natural rate of interest; this is consistent with reduced time preferences.

Although net investment requires a temporary curtailment of possible consumption (i.e., saving), once the consumer goods "come out the pipeline" of the lengthened structure, there will be higher total output than previously. Thus, capitalists refrain from current consumption in the hope of achieving a greater amount of future consumption.

Very specific land factors may suffer a reduced income after a reorganization of the structure of production. Labor, the ultimate nonspecific factor, will generally benefit from increased savings. Ironically, the investors themselves will only enjoy a temporary gain, as the enhanced profits are eroded away by readjusted factor prices.

A *progressing* economy is one in which there are net aggregate profits, a *stationary* economy is one in which aggregate profits equal aggregate losses, and a *retrogressing* economy is one in which losses exceed profits. A progressing economy corresponds to one with net investment, while a retrogressing economy suffers from a reduction in gross investment (i.e., net disinvestment).

When time preferences drop and foster higher investment, this corresponds to a reduction in the natural rate of interest. The reverse is also true. Thus a progressing economy is characterized by falling interest rates, while a retrogressing one is characterized by rising interest rates.

The actual market rate of interest is composed not only of the pure interest rate (due to time preference), but also a component due to the likelihood of default on a loan (or poor returns on a production process).

Risk refers to outcomes that have quantifiable probabilities.

Chapter 8: Production: Entrepreneurship and Change　　　　　*95*

Chapter Outline

1. Entrepreneurial Profit and Loss

In previous chapters, we analyzed the formation of prices in an unhampered, evenly rotating economy. Now we seek to understand the movement of prices in an economy in which the future is not certain. The primary difference is that in the real world (unlike the ERE), the marginal value products of productive factors must be *estimated* by the capitalist-entrepreneurs at the time of hire. There is always the possibility of *erroneous* estimates, and hence the possibility of profit and loss.

Entrepreneurial *profit* occurs when someone buys factors at a certain price and sells the resulting product for a certain price, such that he reaps a higher rate of return than the prevailing rate of interest. Such an entrepreneur has taken advantage of a general *undervaluation* of the particular factors; had others generally been aware of the future sale price of the product, they too would have entered into this market (to earn the higher rate of return). Entrepreneurial loss entails the opposite, in which a capitalist invests in relatively overvalued resources only to find that he can sell the product at a price that does *not* correspond to the rate of interest. (Even if his future revenues exceed his money expenditures on factors, this is still a loss to the capitalist because he could have earned more money by lending his funds out at interest.)

Entrepreneurs tend to eliminate profit and loss opportunities. By investing in those lines offering higher rates of return, they bid up the factor prices and force down the product prices, thus shrinking the rate of return. On the other hand, by fleeing from unprofitable lines, the supply of the final product is reduced (raising its price) while the demand for the relevant factors is reduced (lowering their prices); the net result is a rise in the rate of return. Were all further change ruled out,

96   *Study Guide to Man, Economy, and State with Power and Market*

entrepreneurial profit-seeking would restore a uniform rate of return to all lines corresponding to the prevailing degree of time preference.

Entrepreneurs thus bid up the prices of undervalued factors and reduce the prices of overvalued factors. From the point of view of allocating resources to best satisfy consumer preferences, the profit and loss mechanism serves a definite social function.

2. The Effect of Net Investment

There will be *aggregate* profits in the economy whenever there is net saving and investment, i.e., whenever gross investment exceeds the amount necessary to maintain the previous structure of production. This occurs when investors' time preferences fall, and thus (on the margin) they postpone a greater amount of present consumption in the hope of future consumption. This reduction in present consumption frees up resources (previously used in the lower orders) and allows investment in higher stages of the production structure. The smaller spending on lower stages, coupled with the higher spending on higher stages (and perhaps the introduction of new, higher stages), corresponds to a smaller "markup" between stages. This fall in the natural rate of interest is consistent with the stipulated lower time preferences of investors. Below we graphically illustrate the effects of such a reduction, using Rothbard's specific numbers (pp. 517–18).

In the original structure, gross income is 418 ounces (=100+80+15+60+16+45+12...), total consumption is 100 ounces, and gross investment is the difference, 318 ounces. Of the 100 ounces of net income, 17 go to capitalists while 83 go to land and labor owners. The natural rate of interest is 5 percent at each stage (except for rounding); e.g., the mid-level capitalist spends 45 ounces on an intermediate good, plus

	Income to Land and Labor Factors 83 ounces					
Interest Income 17 ounces	↑	↑	↑	↑	↑	↑
	↑ 19 ounces	↑				
1	← 20	8	↑			
2	← 30	13	↑			
2	← 45	12	↑			
3	← 60	16	↑			
4	← 80		15			
5	← 100 ounces					

Original Structure
(Figure 41 from page 369)

	Income to Land and Labor Factors 69.9 ounces					
Interest Income 10.1 ounces	↑	↑	↑	↑	↑	↑
	↑ 17 ounces	↑				
0.5	← 17.5	10	↑			
0.8	← 28.3	10	↑			
1.1	← 39.4	10	↑			
1.5	← 50.9	11.3	↑			
1.9	← 64.1	1.6	↑			
2.0	← 67.7		10			
2.3	← 80 ounces					

New Structure

98   *Study Guide to Man, Economy, and State with Power and Market*

another 12 on labor and land factors, and then sells the resulting intermediate good for 60 ounces one year later, for a rate of return of 3/57 ≈ 5 percent. Finally, there are six stages of production.

In the second figure, we see the hypothetical structure of production after a net saving and investment of 20 gold ounces. That is, of the original 100 ounces available for consumption, the members of the community decide to spend only 80 on present consumption goods. Thus we know that total consumption must drop to 80, and that gross investment must rise to 338 ounces (318+20). These figures are consistent with the diagram: the bottom row has 80 ounces spent by the consumers on the finished good, while total investment (=67.7+10+64.1+1.6+50.9+11.3…) does indeed (approximately) equal 338. The natural rate of interest in the new arrangement has dropped to 3 percent; e.g., the mid-level capitalist spends 39.4 ounces on a higher-order capital good, plus an additional 10 ounces on labor and land factors, and sells the resulting product one year later for 50.9 ounces, for a rate of return of 1.5/49.4 ≈ 3 percent. Of the total net income of 80 ounces, the capitalists earn 10.1 ounces while the land and labor owners earn the remaining 69.9. (The net income of the capitalists can be found by summing the left-hand column, or by multiplying gross investment by the interest rate; i.e., 338x.03 ≈ 10.1.) Finally, note that there are now seven stages of production; the accumulated savings and corresponding drop in the interest rate have fostered a more "capitalistic" structure of production.

3. Capital Values and Aggregate Profits in a Changing Economy

A *progressing* economy is one in which there are net aggregate profits, a stationary economy is one in which aggregate

Chapter 8: Production: Entrepreneurship and Change 99

profits equal aggregate losses, and a *retrogressing* economy is one in which losses exceed profits. A progressing economy corresponds to one with net investment, while a retrogressing economy suffers from a reduction in gross investment (i.e., net *dis*-investment).

4. Capital Accumulation and the Length of the Structure of Production

Böhm-Bawerk demonstrated that longer, *wisely chosen* processes would always be more *physically* productive than shorter processes. That is, the quantity of physical output from a given input could always be increased by investing the input in a longer process. This of course does *not* mean that *every* longer process will be more physically productive, but merely that there always exists at least one such process (that is both longer and more productive).

5. The Adoption of a New Technique

Other things equal, actors prefer to achieve their consumption goals sooner rather than later. Consequently, they will first exploit the shortest processes, i.e., the ones that involve the least amount of waiting time. The only reason an actor would invest his resources in a longer process is that it promises a greater quantity of output. It is time preference that acts as the ultimate "brake" on engaging in indefinitely lengthy processes. Thus, because of a process of selection, at any given time there are always lengthier, more productive processes "on the shelf," that have not been yet exploited because of the waiting involved. For this reason, new savings (and investment) can *always* yield a higher return to the original factors (after the required delay). Thus capital accumulation alone, even without scientific discoveries or other technological advances, can allow for a continual rise in the standard of living.

6. The Beneficiaries of Saving-Investment

When land and labor factors are invested in lengthier processes, their physical output is greater, leading (eventually) to higher per capita consumption. Net investment (and the corresponding aggregate profits) allow for temporary gains to the investors, but ultimately all increases in productivity will be imputed to the land and labor factors (raising rents and wages).

7. The Progressing Economy and the Pure Rate of Interest

An increase (decrease) in gross investment can only occur because of an antecedent drop (rise) in time preferences, which will also cause a drop (rise) in the pure rate of interest.

8. The Entrepreneurial Component in the Market Interest Rate

In the real world, market rates of interest reflect not merely the underlying "pure" interest rate (due to time preference) as it would exist in the ERE, but also the varying degrees of uncertainty involved in a particular process. For example, a bank might give a loan at 5 percent to a very large firm that has been in business for decades, whereas it might charge 8 percent to a smaller venture that is just opening. This isn't because the bankers have a higher degree of time preference in the latter case, but rather because there is a greater likelihood that the second borrower will default on the loan.

9. Risk, Uncertainty, and Insurance

Following the pioneering treatment by Frank Knight, the distinction between *risk* and *uncertainty* is that risk refers to unknown outcomes with quantifiable probabilities. Risks can be insured against, while uncertainty cannot. All entrepreneurship involves bearing uncertainty; it cannot be transferred away.

Notable Contributions

• To underscore the fallacy of referring to a general "rate of profit," Rothbard invents the concept of a general "rate of loss" (p. 513). His point is that it is *not* normal or automatic to earn profits on the market. The standard excess of product prices over money expenditures on factors is due to *interest*, not entrepreneurship.

• The "paradox of saving" is this: In order to accumulate capital goods and produce a greater volume of output goods, it is necessary to curtail present consumption. But if retailers see a drop in the demand for their products, why would they invest in greater production capabilities for the future? Only with a capital theory (such as the Austrian) that incorporates the role of time in production can one resolve this apparent paradox. As Böhm-Bawerk pointed out in response to a nineteenth-century proponent of this Keynesian view, when people save they are *not* "spending less on consumption," but rather they are spending less on *present* consumption in the hopes of spending *more* on future consumption.

• Rothbard defines the progressing and retrogressing economy in terms of total gross investment, while Mises defined these in terms of *per capita* total investment. (See footnote 16, p. 532.)

Chapter 8: Production: Entrepreneurship and Change 103

Technical Matters

1. On page 510 Rothbard refers to the *money profit* as the "difference between the general interest rate" and the actual rate of return on an investment. This should not be confused with *accounting profit*, which is the excess of money revenues over money expenditures. Often mainstream economists will distinguish between accounting profit and *economic* profit; e.g., a firm could earn a 1 percent accounting profit but actually suffer an economic loss if the rate of interest is 5 percent. The mainstream *economic profit* corresponds to Rothbard's *money profit*. (Rothbard himself is distinguishing between the money corresponding to an economic profit, versus the psychic satisfaction associated with it.)

2. It was an advance in economics to distinguish between *interest* and *profit*. The classical economists (as well as the layman) used *profit* to refer to (what we would call) accounting profit, and thus could not distinguish returns that exceeded the rate due to originary interest.

3. It is important to keep in mind that profits and losses are not merely qualitative, but also quantitative measures of the degree to which entrepreneurs correct (or distort) market prices; e.g., someone who perceives a huge discrepancy in the price structure will reap huge profits, while someone who makes a

minor forecasting error in consumer demand will only suffer minor losses.

4. On pages 523–24, Rothbard writes that in "any equilibrium situation, net saving is zero by definition (since net saving means a change in the level of gross saving over the previous period of time)." These definitions are not entirely compatible with the mainstream approach. For example, standard growth models can certainly have an economy in long-run equilibrium with net investment every period. In this case, net investment would simply mean investment above the amount necessary to cover depreciation, i.e., net investment refers to a growth in the capital stock. Probably the reason for these differing definitions is that Austrians tend to view capital goods as "working capital" or "goods in process," whereas neoclassicals view capital goods almost exclusively as fixed capital: To maintain his output of bread, every period the baker needs to buy more flour, but not a new oven.

Chapter 8: Production: Entrepreneurship and Change 105

Study Questions

1. Can there be profit in the ERE?

2. What might prevent a uniform rate of return in all lines? (p. 514)

3. What happens to factor incomes (both specific and nonspecific) in a progressing economy? (pp. 523–27)

4. Why does a progressing (retrogressing) economy have aggregate profits (losses)? (pp. 532–33)

5. Is the ERE a stationary economy? Is a stationary economy necessarily the ERE? (p. 533)

6. Wouldn't a "capital-saving" invention lead to investment that *shortens* the structure of production? (pp. 540–41)

7. Does a lengthening of the structure of production necessarily involve the adoption of new techniques? (pp. 543–44)

8. Does the rate of interest adjust itself to the supply of capital goods? (pp. 549–50)

9. Can someone really buy "unemployment insurance"? (pp. 552–55)

10. Isn't insurance a form of gambling? (pp. 552–55)

CHAPTER 9

PRODUCTION: PARTICULAR FACTOR PRICES AND PRODUCTIVE INCOMES

Chapter Summary

This chapter analyzes specific factor prices in light of a changing economy. *Rent* is the price paid for the hire of unit services of a factor; the price for a durable factor in its entirety is (in the ERE) equal to the present discounted value of its future rents. In the ERE, only land and labor factors earn net rents. A *wage* is simply the hire price of a unit of labor service.

Taken as a class, the supply of land-in-general is vertical; there are no reservation uses for it. But the supply curves for *particular* uses of land are upward sloping, reflecting the opportunity costs of using a given parcel in alternative ways.

As with land, the supply curves of labor for particular uses will be upward sloping, due to alternative outlets. It is theoretically possible for the supply curve of labor-in-general to be "backwards bending"; i.e., as wage rates reach a certain point, additional rises in the wage rate lead to a *reduction* in the quantity supplied of labor. In contrast to the charges of Keynes, economics does not "assume" full employment. Economics *deduces* that individuals can always "get a job" if they are willing to work for a sufficiently low (possibly negative) wage rate.

Prices determine costs, not vice versa. The plethora of cost curves in mainstream texts assume fixed factor prices, and cannot explain the emergence of prices because they proceed from the viewpoint of an individual, "price taking" firm.

107

A business owner's gross income consists of: (a) interest on capital invested, (b) (implicit) wages for his managerial tasks, (c) rents of ownership-decision, and (outside the ERE) (d) entrepreneurial profit or loss.

If a hypothetical firm were to merge with all other firms, there would no longer be a market for the various factors and hence its owner(s) could not calculate the relative profitability of various lines. Socialism is just a special case of this more general phenomenon.

The same price will emerge for the "same" good, but this is defined from the point of view of the consumers. Thus an orange-in-Florida is not the same good as an orange-in-New-York, and hence the prices for oranges may differ in the two regions.

In contrast to the approach of the classical economists, modern economics recognizes that there is not a two-fold process in which goods are first produced and then "distributed." Rather, goods are produced *and distributed* at the same time; if one alters the incentives facing producers (such as who gets to consume what), then this may upset the total size of the "pie" overall.

Consumer valuations determine the marginal utility of consumer goods, which ultimately determine the prices of these goods. The rental prices of land, labor, and capital factors are then determined on the basis of these prices by computing the DMVP of a productive factor. The pure rate of interest is determined by the time preference schedules of individuals, and this rate is used to compute the asset prices of durable goods, based on their known future rental prices.

Chapter 9: Production: Particular Factor Prices and Productive Incomes   109

Chapter Outline

1. Introduction

This chapter analyzes the effects of a changing economy on specific factor prices.

2. Land, Labor, and Rent

A. Rent

Rent is the price paid for the hire of unit services of a factor; the price for a durable factor in its entirety is (in the ERE) equal to the present discounted value of its future rents. Net rents are equal to gross rents earned minus gross rents paid to owners of factors (necessary to produce a capital good). In the ERE, only land and labor factors earn net rents, because a capital good's gross rent is entirely imputed to the land and labor factors (plus time) necessary for its construction. A *wage* is simply the hire price of a unit of labor service. The capitalized value of the "whole factor" in the labor market implies slavery, and hence cannot exist on a free market. It is an important empirical fact that labor has tended to be scarcer than land; this is why there are always plots of submarginal land but not submarginal ("unemployable") labor.

B. The Nature of Labor

There is no difference between "management" and "labor"; both are hired by the capitalists to perform certain tasks. Yet no one suggests unionizing the vice presidents in various firms to protect them from exploitation.

C. Supply of Land

Taken as a class, the supply of land-in-general is vertical; there are no reservation uses for it. But the supply curves for *particular* uses of land are upward sloping, reflecting the opportunity costs of using a given parcel in alternative ways. To the extent that land (in the economic sense) is permanent, the only reason for "speculative withholding" is that an owner does not wish to commit the land to a present use that would delay its conversion to a more valuable use in the future. This is precisely what the consumers *want* the land speculator to do, contrary to Henry George.

D. Supply of Labor

As with land, the supply curves of labor for particular uses will be upward sloping, due to alternative outlets. However, because labor is the ultimate nonspecific factor, individual supply curves will likely be more elastic than for land factors. It is theoretically possible for the supply curve of labor-in-general to be "backwards bending"; i.e., as wage rates reach a certain point, additional rises in the wage rate lead to a *reduction* in the quantity supplied of labor. This could happen if rising wages lead laborers to consume more leisure.

Wage rates will tend toward equality for equivalent labor units. However, a laborer's total compensation consists of psychic elements as well, which may prevent equalization of *money* wage rates.

E. Productivity and Marginal Productivity

If the supply of capital goods increases, *ceteris paribus* this will increase the MPP of labor and ultimately real

Chapter 9: Production: Particular Factor Prices and Productive Incomes **111**

wages per capita. Thus the rise in real wages over time need not be due to the merits of the workers. For example, an increase in investment in the auto industry will cause the physical product of auto workers to rise (since they work with more and better tools). This will raise wage rates in that industry, which in turn will draw workers from other occupations into it. The reduced supply of workers in, say, the food service industry will raise the equilibrium real wage in it. Hence the cafeteria workers will earn a higher real wage, not because of harder work or training, but because of capitalists investing in auto plants.

F.   A Note on Overt and Total Wage Rates

From the employer's point of view, the total wages he or she pays cannot exceed the worker's DMVP. Thus an increase in pension contributions, health care premiums, or other perks will decrease an employee's take-home pay, *ceteris paribus*.

G.   The "Problem" of Unemployment

In contrast to the charges of Keynes, economics does not "assume" full employment. Economics deduces that individuals can always "get a job" if they are willing to work for a sufficiently low (possibly negative) wage rate. Thus it is not jobs that are the goal, but high-paying jobs, and in order to achieve this goal we need capital accumulation (to raise the DMVP of labor), not government "pump priming."

3. Entrepreneurship and Income

A. Costs to the Firm

Prices determine costs, not vice versa. (Recall that the "costs of production" are largely the *prices* of factors.) The plethora of cost curves in mainstream texts assume fixed factor prices, and cannot explain the emergence of prices because they proceed from the viewpoint of an individual, "price taking" firm.

Average costs per unit may vary with the level of output because of indivisibilities in factor inputs.

B. Business Income

A business owner's gross income consists of: (a) interest on capital invested, (b) (implicit) wages for his managerial tasks, (c) rents of ownership-decision, and (outside the ERE) (d) entrepreneurial profit or loss.

C. Personal Consumer Service

Certain entrepreneurs (such as doctors and lawyers) sell their labor directly to the final consumer. These people are self-employed and earn a wage only in the implicit sense.

D. Market Calculation and Implicit Earnings

Implicit earnings can only be computed if there are *explicit* prices on an actual market with which to compare one's gross income from a given activity.

Chapter 9: Production: Particular Factor Prices and Productive Incomes **113**

E. Vertical Integration and the Size of the Firm

If a hypothetical firm were to merge with all other firms, there would no longer be a market for the various factors and hence its owner(s) could not calculate the relative profitability of various lines. Such a chaotic situation would never persist on a free market. Socialism is just a special (important) case of this more general phenomenon.

4. The Economics of Location and Spatial Relations

The same price will emerge for the "same" good, but this is defined from the point of view of the consumers. Thus an orange-in-Florida is not the same good as an orange-in-New-York, and hence the prices for oranges may differ in the two regions. Production centers will not be located merely on the basis of technical efficiency; the cost of transporting the goods to the final consumers must also be considered. Also, the money wage rates in an area with a high "cost of living" may adjust accordingly.

5. A Note on the Fallacy of "Distribution"

In contrast to the approach of the classical economists (particularly Ricardo), modern economics recognizes that there is not a two-fold process in which goods are first produced and then "distributed." Rather, goods are produced *and distributed* at the same time; if one alters the incentives facing producers (such as who gets to consume what), then this may upset the total size of the "pie" overall. It is true that richer individuals have a greater say in determining the course of production, but their greater wealth is itself a result of prior market activities. On a free market, all wealth is achieved through prior acts of homesteading, production, or receipt of a gift.

6. A Summary of the Market

In the ERE, the Austrian economist can explain the height of all market prices in a logical fashion. Consumer valuations determine the marginal utility of consumer goods, which ultimately determine the prices of these goods. The rental prices of land, labor, and capital factors are then determined on the basis of these prices, and the technological recipes of production, by computing the DMVP of a productive factor. The pure rate of interest is determined by the time preference schedules of individuals, and this rate is used to compute the capitalized present value (i.e., asset price) of durable goods, based on their known future rental prices.

Outside the ERE, actual market prices will *tend* toward these final values. Uncertainty due to changing conditions will always leave open the possibility for forecasting errors. Profits will accrue to those entrepreneurs who best deploy scarce resources for the satisfaction of consumer desires.

Chapter 9: Production: Particular Factor Prices and Productive Incomes **115**

Notable Contributions

• Although he mentions his debt to Böhm-Bawerk, Rothbard's discussion of "ultimate-decision-making ability" (pp. 602–03) is fairly unique.

• Rothbard takes care to distinguish the Austrian view of rent and cost from the Marshallian notion of "quasi-rents" (pp. 558–59) and the typical mainstream obsession with cost curves (pp. 588–92).

• Rothbard generalized Mises's calculation argument to show that it applies even to "private" integration of industries (p. 615).

Technical Matters

1. Some economists argue that the case of a backward bending supply curve of labor is an example of the elusive "Giffen good." If we define the price of the good *leisure* as the wage rate, then a backward bending supply curve would mean that (at least in certain regions) a higher price of leisure leads to consumers buying more of it, an apparent violation of the Law of Demand for the leisure good.

2. The "market socialists" responded to Mises's challenge by showing how, with the stipulated technologies, resource supplies, and consumer preferences, a central planner could identify optimal production plans using Walrasian analysis. Hayek admitted that this solution was valid in theory, but claimed that practically it would be impossible to implement due to the volume of equations, and the difficulty of actually transmitting the relevant knowledge to the planners. Rothbard and others have rejected this "concession" and insist that even in principle, the central planners could not calculate without market prices for the means of production.

3. Someone like Keynes would object to Rothbard's claims (pp. 581–88) that large-scale unemployment is impossible on a free market, and that more workers can always be hired at lower wage rates. Keynes argues in the *General Theory* that this "classical" (his term) view overlooks the empirical fact of widespread "involuntary" unemployment during the 1930s, and that it overlooks the possibility that workers in the aggregate will be unable to lower their *real* wage

Chapter 9: Production: Particular Factor Prices and Productive Incomes 117

demands. Roughly, Keynes argues that any individual worker can agree to work for lower money wages (and hence real wages), but if *all* workers agree to, say, a 10 percent wage cut, then this lowers the amount of purchasing power in the hands of consumers, and prices may also fall by a large amount; hence the real wage of the workers may not fall. (Of course this note is not meant to endorse Keynes's analysis.)

Study Questions

1. Rothbard says that a rising population will, on the one hand, tend to lower wages because of falling MVP, but that this tendency can be overcome by the enhanced division of labor. Does the same apply to capital goods? Is there an "optimum" amount of capital goods? (pp. 561–62)

2. Could there be a backward supply curve for a land factor? (p. 574)

3. Rothbard says that "psychic wage rates will be equalized . . . being equal to money wage rates plus or minus a psychic benefit or *psychic* disutility component" (p. 576). Does this principle involve an interpersonal utility comparison?

4. Rothbard says that a small scale firm may not be able to compete with a larger one when using a machine below its efficient scale of output. But why isn't there an analogous problem for a big firm forced to operate machinery *above* its ideal output level? (p. 597)

5. Why would someone earn a rent for his "ultimate-decision-making ability" even in the ERE? (p. 604)

6. Why does Rothbard classify a servant as self-employed? (p. 605)

Chapter 9: Production: Particular Factor Prices and Productive Incomes   *119*

7. Suppose a firm can buy a third-order good for $100 and sell the *first*-order good two years later for $121, and that each stage of production takes exactly one year. Suppose further that second-order goods sell for $115. If the rate of interest is 10 percent, is this firm maximizing its profit? (pp. 610–11)

8. Could a certain city be identical to another, except that all money prices were double in the former? After all, doesn't Rothbard argue that money wage rates adjust for differences in the prices of various consumer goods? (p. 619)

9. If a certain manufacturing plant is located closer to a population center, does that mean its owners will earn higher profits than the owners of a plant located farther away? What if we further stipulate that the production technologies are identical? (p. 622)

10. Why must one *first* determine the rate of interest before computing prices of tractors? (p. 625)

CHAPTER 10

MONOPOLY AND COMPETITION

Chapter Summary

Consumer preferences ultimately drive a market economy; many have termed this outcome as "consumers' sovereignty." Yet this is an inappropriate political metaphor; on a free market, *individuals* have complete control over their bodies and other property.

Cartels allegedly restrict output below the socially optimum level. But consider the "worst case" where a cartel destroys some of its product. Even here, the true "waste" is not the destroyed product, but rather the scarce resources that went into the production of the excess units; once the cartel produces the profit-maximizing amount in the future, these resources will be channeled elsewhere. Moreover, the formation of a cartel in the first place is quite similar to the founding of a corporation or a merger, yet many view only the cartel as inefficient.

In a free market, firms will tend to be the optimum size. Lower unit costs of large-scale production will tend to increase firm size, but the overhead costs of bureaucracy eventually check this trend. The ultimate limit is the chaos that would ensue if a firm eliminated the market prices for its inputs and products. Voluntary cartels formed for the purpose of restricting output and raising prices are inherently unstable. There will always be an incentive to cheat on the cartel agreement and produce more than the assigned quota. Even if the members of the

121

cartel can reach an agreement and obey it, if they are truly earning "above normal" returns, outsiders will enter the industry.

A monopoly may be defined as (1) a single seller of a good or service, (2) the recipient of a government privilege, or (3) a business unit that can achieve monopoly prices. The first definition is vacuous; *everyone* is a monopolist in this sense. The second definition is legitimate, and focuses on government intervention that hampers welfare. The third definition is empty once we realize there is no such thing as "monopoly price." Simply put, there is no such *thing* as a "monopoly price" to which we can contrast a "competitive price"; there is no way we can even in principle define these concepts. All we can discuss is the unhampered price that would emerge on a free market.

Although a union presents a coherent example of restriction of output and the achievement of higher prices, this is *not* an example of monopoly; the privileged workers gain at the expense of nonunion members. A typical argument for unions is that the marginal productivity determination of wage rates, in practice, leads not to a unique value but rather a *zone* of possible wage rates. The problem with such a justification is that such zones of indeterminacy shrink as more and more people enter the market. Moreover, in practice unions often rely on the actual use (or at least threat) of violence to achieve such "bargains" with management.

The crucial characteristic of a "perfectly competitive" industry is that each firm perceives the demand for its product as a horizontal line. Yet this is clearly absurd; even in theory, all demand curves must be downward sloping. The claims of "excess capacity" in monopolistically competitive industries defy rationality and ultimately rely on geometrical tricks: Once we drop the assumption of smooth cost curves, the argument falls apart.

Chapter 10: Monopoly and Competition

Chapter Outline

1. The Concept of Consumers' Sovereignty

A. Consumers' Sovereignty versus Individual Sovereignty

Consumer preferences ultimately drive a market economy; many have termed this outcome as "consumers' sovereignty." Yet this is an inappropriate political metaphor; on a free market, *individuals* have complete control over their bodies and other property. Consumers can't force producers to make certain goods; they can merely try to influence producers (to the extent that they seek monetary returns) by their spending decisions.

B. Professor Hutt and Consumers' Sovereignty

Hutt's treatment is the most comprehensive and yet is riddled with problems. Consumers truly exercise "sovereignty" over production only if we treat certain decisions by producers (when they pass up higher revenues in order to achieve psychic satisfaction) as implicit acts of consumption. In this formal sense, then, "consumption" always rules production decisions—but this isn't a useful way to approach the exchange relations on a market. In any event, Hutt inconsistently drops the tautologous approach and then holds up consumers' sovereignty, not as a necessary condition, but rather as an *ideal benchmark* against which to compare the actual economy.

2. Cartels and Their Consequences

A. Cartels and "Monopoly Price"

The alleged evil of a cartel is that it restricts output and thus hampers the achievement of consumers' sovereignty. But consider the "worst case" scenario of a cartel that actually destroys product in order to increase its profit. Clearly the excess production was a *mistake* that will tend not to be repeated; even a cartel would rather produce the amount it intended to sell, rather than overproduce and then destroy the excess. The true "waste" then is *not* the destroyed product, but rather the scarce resources that went into the production of the excess units; once the cartel produces the profit-maximizing amount in the future, these resources will be channeled elsewhere.

B. Cartels, Mergers, and Corporations

Those who criticize cartels generally do not view mergers, let alone the formation of a corporation, as sinister or inefficient; but what is the essential difference between these events and the formation of a (voluntary) cartel?

C. Economics, Technology, and the Size of the Firm

In a free market, firms will tend to be the optimum (from the consumers' point of view) size. On the one hand, lower unit costs of large-scale production will tend to increase firm size, but on the other, the overhead costs of bureaucracy eventually check this trend. The ultimate limit is the chaos that would ensue if a firm eliminated the market prices for its inputs and products.

Chapter 10: Monopoly and Competition

D. The Instability of the Cartel

Voluntary cartels (i.e., those not supported by government restriction) formed for the purpose of restricting output and raising prices are inherently unstable. First, there will always be an incentive to cheat on the cartel agreement and produce more than the assigned quota. Second, the more efficient members will demand larger and larger quotas over time; why should they restrict their own output in order to benefit inefficient competitors? Third, even if the members of the cartel can reach an agreement and obey it, if they are truly earning "above normal" returns, outsiders will enter the industry.

E. Free Competition and Cartels

Some critics allege that cartels restrict the "freedom" of the consumer by eliminating choices. But this argument confuses *freedom* with *power* (of choice). Another argument is that certain industries have such high startup costs that this "entry barrier" allows for long-run profits. But no individual needs to come up with $20 million to enter the automobile industry; a large number of individuals can pool their assets by forming a corporation.

F. The Problem of One Big Cartel

The fear of a giant cartel overlooks the calculation problem. Moreover, why hasn't a giant cartel emerged on the (relatively) free market already?

3. The Illusion of Monopoly Price

A. Definitions of Monopoly

A monopoly may be defined as (1) a single seller of a good or service, (2) the recipient of a government privilege, or (3) a business unit that can achieve monopoly prices. The first definition is vacuous; *everyone* is a monopolist in this sense. The second definition is legitimate, and focuses on government intervention that hampers welfare. The third definition is empty once we realize there is no such thing as "monopoly price."

B. The Neoclassical Theory of Monopoly Price

The neoclassical theory of monopoly assumes that there is some identifiable "competitive" price and level of output with which to contrast the "monopolistic" price and output.

C. Consequences of Monopoly-Price Theory

Even if neoclassical monopoly theory were valid, the standard, sinister conclusions would not necessarily follow. Such monopolists would still be subject to the consumers' voluntary spending decisions, and there would be no lasting monopoly "profits," but rather monopoly *gains* imputed to certain factors of production.

D. The Illusion of Monopoly Price on the Unhampered Market

Simply put, there is no such *thing* as a "monopoly price" to which we can contrast a "competitive price"; there is no way we can even in principle define these

Chapter 10: Monopoly and Competition

concepts. All we can discuss is the unhampered price that would emerge on a free market.

E. Some Problems in the Theory of the Illusion of Monopoly Price

Certain "obvious" cases—such as so-called location and natural monopolies—may make the preceding section's arguments appear incredible. Yet even in these cases, a careful analysis shows that either there are monopolies everywhere (in which case the concept is vacuous), or there are no monopolies (in which case it is irrelevant). Only when the government grants a privilege backed up by force is the concept of monopoly significant.

4. Labor Unions

A. Restrictionist Pricing of Labor

Although a union presents a coherent example of restriction of output and the achievement of higher prices, this is *not* an example of monopoly; the privileged workers gain at the expense of nonunion members.

B. Some Arguments for Unions: A Critique

A typical argument for unions is that the marginal productivity determination of wage rates, in practice, leads not to a unique value but rather a *zone* of possible wage rates. In this view, the union's function is to use its collective bargaining power to achieve a wage rate on the high end of the zone of mutually advantageous wages. The problem with such a justification is that such zones of indeterminacy shrink as more and more people enter the market. Moreover, in practice unions often rely on the actual use (or at least threat) of violence to achieve such "bargains" with management.

5. The Theory of Monopolistic or Imperfect Competition

A. Monopolistic Competitive Price

The crucial characteristic of a "perfectly competitive" industry is that each firm perceives the demand for its product as a horizontal (i.e., perfectly elastic) line. Yet this is clearly absurd; even in theory, all demand curves must be downward sloping (though they may possess vertical drops). Another alleged difference is that perfectly competitive firms may disregard the response of their competitors to their own pricing and output decisions, whereas an oligopolist cannot. But this too is spurious: The demand curve, by definition, relates hypothetical prices to the quantities consumers will purchase. If lowering the price causes rivals to react in a certain way, the demand curve already contains this information.

B. The Paradox of Excess Capacity

Because of low entry barriers, in the long run there is zero economic profit in a monopolistically competitive industry; at the equilibrium output level, each firm's price is just equal to average total cost. But because demand curves are downward sloping, by simple geometry this implies that each firm will set output at a level *below* that which minimizes ATC. Apparently, then, monopolistic competition leads to aggregate inefficiencies in production.

Chapter 10: Monopoly and Competition   129

Yet this theory makes no sense. Why would firms deliberately construct factories that operate at lowest cost *above* the long-run planned level of output? The basic trick of the neoclassical argument relies on geometry, not economics. If we drop the assumption of smooth cost curves, it is no problem reconciling a downward sloping demand curve with operation at minimum ATC.

C. Chamberlin and Selling Cost

There is no important distinction between production and selling costs. Advertising does not "create" consumer demands for products that people don't really "need." On a free market, consumers are free to spend their money however they wish.

6. Multiform Prices and Monopoly

Once we take into account transactions costs, it is possible for multiple prices to exist even for "the same" good. However, this is not an infringement on consumers' sovereignty; some consumers would rather risk paying higher prices in exchange for not spending time researching all relevant sellers.

7. Patents and Copyrights

On a free market, there would be no analogue to the patent; someone who independently discovers a technological recipe would be free to begin using it immediately. However, there *would* be copyrights, in the sense that it would be illegal to fraudulently impersonate another individual when selling a good or service.

130   Study Guide to Man, Economy, and State with Power and Market

Notable Contributions

• Rothbard's critique of the concept of consumers' sovereignty is quite pioneering. Even Mises adopted the term (though Rothbard would view his treatment as more satisfactory than Hutt's).

• His defense of cartels and his critique of the theory of monopoly price are some of Rothbard's finest contributions to economics.

• Rothbard's distinction between patents and copyrights was also quite revolutionary, although recent work (e.g., Stephan Kinsella's) has questioned even the defense of copyright.

Chapter 10: Monopoly and Competition

Technical Matters

1. In his critique of the fear of monopoly, Rothbard says that consumers "benefit from the resulting voluntary exchanges" (p. 634), and that "if the resulting exchanges really hurt them, consumers would boycott the 'monopolistic' firm" (p. 635). He also points out that the motives of alleged monopolists are no different from the motives of any other producer. Although true, these particular responses would not satisfy a mainstream economist. The claim is not that consumers would be better off with no producer at all (rather than a monopolist), but rather that monopoly is bad compared to the case of a perfectly competitive market. Moreover, the standard mainstream economist does not attribute sinister motives to the monopolist; he concedes that the perfectly competitive firm seeks to maximize profits just as the monopolist does. The alleged difference, however, is that the market structure in the case of competition leads the selfish producers to set output at the "optimal" level, i.e., where P=MC, whereas the monopolist (because of a falling demand curve) sets output where P>MC. (Of course Rothbard later deals with these arguments.)

2. Almost all of mainstream industrial organization theory relies on the assumption of a single price for all units. But as Rothbard points out (p. 641), the alleged "deadweight loss" of producing where P>MC could always be avoided if the firms with market power were able to cut side deals with consumers and sell additional units at lower prices. Organizations such as Sam's Club, which charges a flat membership fee

132   *Study Guide to Man, Economy, and State with Power and Market*

and then charges very low unit prices, show that this type of arrangement is not a mere theoretical curiosity.

3. On page 660 and pp. 689–90, Rothbard argues that demand is always elastic above the free market price. However, a mainstream economist would respond that Rothbard is conflating the market demand curve with the individual firm's "perceived" demand curve; the market demand for wheat may be inelastic at the "competitive" price, even though individual wheat farmers perceive perfectly elastic demand curves. (Of course Rothbard criticizes such a view elsewhere in the chapter.)

Chapter 10: Monopoly and Competition   *133*

Study Questions

1. How are anticartelists proposing a caste system? (pp. 640–41)

2. In what sense could Tiger Woods be considered a monopolist?

3. In New York City, cab drivers must obtain a medallion from the government in order to legally operate. Does such a restriction allow cabbies to earn long-run profits? (p. 679)

4. Why might a large firm be at a disadvantage in a "cutthroat" price war with a small competitor? (p. 684)

5. If a firm is caught selling "below costs," isn't this proof of strategic behavior designed to hurt its competitors rather than simply pleasing customers? (p. 687)

6. Rothbard rejects the coherence of a "competitive" price because it cannot be distinguished from the free market price. But what about, say, the pure rate of interest? In practice, the Austrian can't tell what portion of the actual market rate of interest is due to time preference, risk, inflation, etc. (pp. 696–97)

7. Could there be a voluntary union that achieves a restriction in output and higher wages for union members? (p. 711)

8. On page 717, Rothbard argues that even if a zone of indeterminacy in wages exists, competition among employers will tend to push wages up to the maximum value in this range. But is this just another way of saying that there will be no zone at all?

9. On pages 739–40, Rothbard characterizes a seller's behavior as an implicit act of consumption. Is this consistent with his earlier critique (footnote 2, page 630) of Hutt's attempt to use a similar tactic in discussing consumer sovereignty?

10. In Rothbard's view, how might it be a crime to take a video camera into a theater in order to produce a "bootleg" copy of a blockbuster? What contracts are being violated here?

CHAPTER 11

MONEY AND ITS PURCHASING POWER

Chapter Summary

Like all goods, the price of money is determined by the interaction between supply and demand. Money is unique in that its "price" is not a single number—in this sense the price of an ounce of gold would always be *one* (oz. gold). Rather, the price of a unit of money is an entire *vector* of the money commodity's exchange ratios with units of every other good and service available on the market. The purchasing power of money (PPM) is thus its "price." At any given time, all units of money are in someone's possession, i.e., comprise part of someone's *cash balance*. There is no such thing as money "in circulation." Thus it is arbitrary to denounce "hoarding."

If the demand for money increases, this means that people wish to hold a stock of money balances higher than the actual stock in existence. This "shortage" of money balances can be eliminated through a rise in the PPM of money. A similar analysis holds for a drop in the demand for money. If the total stock of money changes, the PPM also adjusts until the quantity demanded of money equals the size of the new stock. The total stock of money increases with mining, etc., but decreases through wear and tear, and as the money commodity is devoted to industrial or consumption purposes.

Money is useful only insofar as it possesses purchasing power. Other things equal, it is always better to have more producer or

135

consumer goods. In contrast, any stock of money can fully perform the functions of a medium of exchange.

Money would fade out of use in the ERE. With perfect certainty, people would loan out their cash balances and schedule repayment just in time for their planned expenditures.

The PPM and the rate of interest are not inherently connected. For example, the demand for money could increase (raising the PPM), yet if time preferences remain the same, this will not affect the (real) rate of interest.

New money always enters the economy at specific points; contrary to typical thought experiments, it is never the case that everyone's cash balance suddenly increases by a certain percentage. Even in such an unrealistic scenario, money would still be "non-neutral": Some people would spend their new money more quickly than others, and thus would experience a relative gain as the PPM adjusted to the new stock.

If there are two or more commonly accepted media of exchange, their exchange ratio will be such that no arbitrage opportunities are available in selling the moneys against other goods. This is termed *purchasing power parity*. For example, if an ounce of gold buys 1,000 DVDs while an ounce of platinum buys 2,500, then the equilibrium exchange rate must be 2.5 ounces of gold for 1 ounce of platinum.

Money is not a measure of value. When someone buys a TV for $50, we cannot conclude that he "values it" at $50; on the contrary we know that he values the TV *more* than he valued the $50. All price indices are arbitrary.

In reaction to the wild swings of the PPM (caused by government), many economists propose various schemes to "stabilize" the PPM. Yet such proposals are undesirable and unworkable.

Chapter 11: Money and Its Purchasing Power 137

Chapter Outline

1. Introduction

Earlier chapters dealt with the emergence of money out of barter, and the formation of money prices. In the present chapter we analyze the impact changes in the money relation have upon the (unhampered) market.

2. The Money Relation: The Demand for and the Supply of Money

Like all goods, the price of money is determined by the interaction between supply and demand. Money is unique in that its "price" is not a single number—in this sense the price of an ounce of gold would always be *one* (oz. gold). Rather, the price of a unit of money is an entire *vector* of the money commodity's exchange ratios with units of every other good and service available on the market. The purchasing power of money (PPM) is thus its "price."

The total demand for money consists of (1) the *exchange demand* for money (by sellers of all other goods who wish to purchase money) and (2) the *reservation demand* (by those who already hold money). As with all goods, the demand curve for money is downward sloping: as the PPM falls, people will demand a greater quantity of the money commodity.

At any given time, all units of money are in someone's possession, i.e., comprise part of someone's *cash balance*. There is no such thing as money "in circulation." Thus it is arbitrary to denounce "hoarding."

The *supply* of money at any given time is a vertical line; regardless of the PPM, there are just so many units of money in the economy. (Remember that we are using the total demand/total stock analysis.) The equilibrium PPM is then determined

138   *Study Guide to Man, Economy, and State with Power and Market*

by the intersection of the total demand curve with the given total stock.

3. Changes in the Money Relation

If the demand for money increases, this means that people wish to hold a stock of money balances higher than the actual stock in existence. This "shortage" of money balances can be eliminated through a rise in the PPM of money; that is, if people want to hold higher money balances, they stop spending as liberally and thus the nominal money prices of other goods and services fall until equilibrium is reestablished. (Recall that people ultimately care about their *real* cash balances; a given nominal stock of money can represent any desired real cash balance with the appropriate PPM.) A similar analysis holds for a drop in the demand for money. If the total stock of money changes, the PPM also adjusts until the quantity demanded of money equals the size of the new stock.

4. Utility of the Stock of Money

In its capacity as a medium of exchange, money is useful only insofar as it possesses purchasing power. If producer or consumer goods were available for free, this would be a tremendous boon to humanity. But if money has a zero price, it is useless. Other things equal, it is always better to have more producer or consumer goods. In contrast, any stock of money can fully perform the functions of a medium of exchange. Increasing the money stock (aside from its nonmonetary uses) can't make the community richer per capita; it can only redistribute wealth.

5. The Demand for Money

A. Money in the ERE and in the Market

Money would fade out of use in the ERE. With perfect certainty, people would loan out their cash balances and schedule repayment just in time for their planned expenditures. But if everyone is doing this, then the demand for money (i.e., the desire to hold cash balances) would be virtually nonexistent. In the real world of uncertainty, "idle" cash balances perform a useful service, as they are a means to cope with unplanned expenditures.

B. Speculative Demand

People's demand for money may be influenced by their speculation about future changes in the PPM. For example, if a woman expects that prices in general will rise greatly in a few months, this may lower her current demand for money (i.e., she will spend more). Thus her expectation of a future fall in the PPM will lead to a reduction in the current PPM of money.

C. Secular Influences on the Demand for Money

As an economy grows, there are more exchange opportunities and hence (*ceteris paribus*) an increase in the demand for money. On the other hand, the development of clearing systems reduces the demand for cash.

D. Demand for Money Unlimited?

Some reject the notion of a demand for money, because "people always want more money." Yet this is true for *all* producer and consumer goods! It is simply not true that people always want more *money* (cash); indeed, anyone who owns any nonmonetary asset demonstrates that he or she does *not* want "more money."

E. The PPM and the Rate of Interest

The PPM and the rate of interest are not inherently connected. For example, the demand for money could increase (raising the PPM), yet if time preferences remain the same, this will not affect the (real) rate of interest. Instead, each person could increase his cash balances by reducing expenditures on present *and* future goods in a proportion reflecting the original time preference.

F. Hoarding and the Keynesian System

"Hoarding" is a great evil in the Keynesian view. In this approach, macro equilibrium is achieved when two necessary conditions are satisfied: One the one hand, total income must of course equal total expenditures (since one man's expenditure is another man's income); this necessity corresponds to the 45-degree line on a graph. On the other hand, any individual's expenditures are a certain *function* of income; at zero income, a person still needs to eat, and so there is a small expenditure. Then for every additional dollar of income, the person spends only a fraction of it. Thus an individual's expenditure (graphed as a function of income) is a line with a positive intercept and slope between zero and one. The same holds for the community, and where the community's line intersects the 45-degree line determines the equilibrium amount of income.

The unique feature of the Keynesian system was that this macro equilibrium could occur at a level where real

Chapter 11: Money and Its Purchasing Power   *141*

output was less than necessary for "full employment." In order to induce employers to hire more workers, the community needed to spend more and save less (thus increasing the slope of the expenditure line, so that it intersected the 45-degree line farther to the right).

The fundamental flaw with such reasoning is that there can only be unemployment if wage rates are higher than the market clearing level. This can occur either through union pressure or government edict. Only if we assume that workers do care about *money* (rather than real) wages could hoarding have such sinister effects.

G. The Purchasing-Power and Terms-of-Trade Components in the Rate of Interest

Following Irving Fisher's canonical treatment, it is standard to explain the nominal interest rate as the real rate of interest plus a "purchasing power" component. For example, if price inflation is 5 percent and the real interest rate is 5 percent, then (Fisher would argue) the nominal interest rate will be 10 percent, because lenders need to be compensated for the decline in the PPM of their money during the time of the loan. One grave problem with this is that (obviously) the nominal rate can never be *negative*, and so Fisher's explanation can't be the whole story in times of severe price deflation. Moreover, to the extent that future changes in prices are fully anticipated, *present* prices will adjust. "The purchasing power component, then, is *not* the reflection, as has been thought, of *expectations* of changes in purchasing power. It is the reflection of the change itself" (p. 797).

142   *Study Guide to Man, Economy, and State with Power and Market*

6. The Supply of Money

A. The Stock of the Money Commodity

The total stock of money increases with mining, etc., but decreases through wear and tear, and as the money commodity is devoted to industrial or consumption purposes.

B. Claims to Money: The Money Warehouse

A warehouse may issue certificates entitling the bearer to a certain good stored in the warehouse. If the community has no reason to doubt the reliability of redemption, the certificates may circulate as *goods-substitutes*. In the case of money, the warehouse may realize that it can issue a greater number of certificates than it can redeem; this is "fractional reserve banking" (FRB), and explains banks' current susceptibility to "runs." In a free market, FRB would be illegal because of its fraudulent nature.

C. Money-Substitutes and the Supply of Money

Because the public may accept money-substitutes as readily as the original money commodity, they are a commonly accepted medium of exchange and hence must be classified as money. "Money in the broader sense" refers to the total supply of money (including money certificates) in people's cash balances, while "money proper" or "standard money" refers only to the supply of the original money commodity.

Under 100-percent reserve banking, deposits in the banking system do not influence the total supply of

Chapter 11: Money and Its Purchasing Power   *143*

money, but merely change its composition (between certificates and money proper). Under FRB, however, the deposit of money proper can lead to an increase in the overall supply of money.

D. A Note on Some Criticisms of 100-Percent Reserve

Under 100-percent reserve, banks could still earn an income by charging for their warehouse services (i.e., checking accounts). They could still operate as credit intermediaries by borrowing from individuals (i.e., savings accounts) and lending the funds to borrowers at a higher interest rate. This latter activity is consistent with 100-percent reserve banking because the deposited funds are *not* the lenders' money for the duration of the loan; the depositor (into a savings account) has sold present money for future money.

7. Gains and Losses During a Change in the Money Relation

New money always enters the economy at specific points; contrary to typical thought experiments, it is never the case that everyone's cash balance suddenly increases by a certain percentage. Even in such an unrealistic scenario, money would still be "non-neutral": Some people would spend their new money more quickly than others, and thus would experience a relative gain as the PPM adjusted to the new stock.

8. The Determination of Prices: The Goods Side and the Money Side

The ultimate determinants of the PPM are: (1) the stock of all goods, (2) the reservation demand for money, (3) the stock

144   *Study Guide to Man, Economy, and State with Power and Market*

of money, and (4) the reservation demand for goods. The first two determinants increase the PPM, while the latter two decrease it.

9. Interlocal Exchange

A. Uniformity of the Geographic Purchasing Power of Money

As with all goods, the money commodity will tend to have one price in the market. Some allege that the PPM of money can differ from region to region; is not the price of a movie higher in New York than in Boise? Yet a movie in New York is not the same good as one in Boise.

B. Clearing in Interlocal Exchange

The use of clearing houses greatly facilitates interregional trade. If French consumers had to ship gold to Russia every time they wished to buy a Russian good, and vice versa, then there would be a lower volume of trade. In contrast, with clearing only the *net* surplus of gold needs to be shipped from one country to the other.

10. Balances of Payments

An individual's "balance of payments" must always be in balance, so long as cash balances and credit transactions are included. In general an individual will always have huge "trade deficits" with the owners of retail shops and huge "trade surpluses" with his employer. The balance of payments for an entire nation is simply the aggregation of all the individual citizens' balances of payments.

Chapter 11: Money and Its Purchasing Power   *145*

11. Monetary Attributes of Goods

A. Quasi Money

Some goods (such as jewels and high-grade deben-
tures) are very liquid and hence function as quasi money.
However, they are not actually money because they cannot be used to settle debts at par. Nonetheless, their high
marketability raises their demand even further, and
investment in them will carry a lower rate of return.

B. Bills of Exchange

Bills of exchange are credit instruments, not money
substitutes.

12. Exchange Rates of Coexisting Money

If there are two or more commonly accepted media of
exchange, their exchange ratio will be such that no arbitrage
opportunities are available in selling the moneys against other
goods. This is termed *purchasing power parity*. For example, if an
ounce of gold buys 1,000 DVDs while an ounce of platinum
buys 2,500, then the equilibrium exchange rate must be 2.5
ounces of gold for 1 ounce of platinum.

13. The Fallacy of the Equation of Exchange

The holistic approach to money is epitomized in the equation of exchange, $MV=PT$. This is an identity that states that the
number of money units multiplied by the average rate of
turnover ("velocity"), must equal the average price times the
number of transactions. Apart from its lack of subjective marginal theory, there are grave flaws with this approach. The concepts of velocity and average price are completely empty; they
are really just placeholders necessary to fill out the equation.

14. The Fallacy of Measuring and Stabilizing the PPM

A. Measurement

Money is not a measure of value. When someone buys a TV for $50, we cannot conclude that he "values it" at $50; on the contrary we know that he values the TV *more* than he valued the $50. All price indices are arbitrary.

B. Stabilization

In reaction to the wild swings of the PPM (caused by government), many economists propose various schemes to "stabilize" the PPM. Yet such proposals are undesirable and unworkable. In any event, if businesspeople really wanted to substitute a basket of commodities as the standard unit of account (rather than the money commodity), they could do so in their contracts.

15. Business Fluctuations

Particular businesses may fail because of entrepreneurial misjudgment. But during the bust phase of the "business cycle," we see evidence of widespread error. This cannot occur on an unhampered market; its explanation will be postponed until the next chapter.

16. Schumpeter's Theory of Business Cycles

Schumpeter's explanation of the business cycle, though better than many others, suffers from its reliance on overlapping cycles, and it ultimately lays the blame on innovation. But Schumpeter doesn't explain why there should be sudden *clusters* of innovation that trigger the boom-bust cycle.

17. Further Fallacies of the Keynesian System

A. Interest and Investment

The interest rate has no causal relation to investment; both are determined by time preferences.

B. The "Consumption Function"

In contrast to investment, Keynesians consider consumption a very "stable" function of income, and find a high correlation between the two. But since consumption is a very large fraction of income, it is no wonder! If instead Keynesians had run regressions comparing income with investment, and income with *saving*, they would not have classified investment as "unstable."

C. The Multiplier

Using the exact same logic as the Keynesians, one could "prove" that the way to boost GDP by $100,000 is to give the reader an extra dollar bill.

18. The Fallacy of the Acceleration Principle

The so-called acceleration principle is best illustrated with an example: If a laundromat has ten dryers with an average life of ten years, then on average the owner will buy a new dryer every year. If his business picks up 10 percent, such that he needs to carry eleven dryers, he will have to buy two additional dryers in the first year—an increase of 100 percent. Hence the increased consumer demand has been "accelerated" by a factor of ten in the higher orders. But as Hutt first pointed out, such scenarios completely rely on the time period under consideration. If we adopt a ten-year framework, then there is no

148   *Study Guide to Man, Economy, and State with Power and Market*

"acceleration" at all: a 10 percent increase in business translates into a 10 percent increase in sales for the producers of industrial dryers.

Chapter 11: Money and Its Purchasing Power   *149*

Notable Contributions

• Rothbard's critique of the Fisher relation (which equates the nominal interest rate with the real rate plus a purchasing power component) is quite unorthodox yet irresistible.

• The discussion of free coinage and 100-percent reserve banking (pp. 799–811) anticipate much of the modern Austro-libertarian literature.

• Rothbard's critiques of Fisher's equation of exchange (pp. 831–42), and various Keynesian concepts (pp. 859–68) are simply brilliant, and should put to rest the frequent allegation that Austrians are incapable of mathematical reasoning.

Technical Matters

1. When Rothbard decomposes the total demand for money into the "exchange demand" and the "reservation demand" (p. 756), the former technically includes the nonmonetary demand for the money commodity (p. 760). For example, someone who sells labor services in order to acquire gold for use as fillings in his teeth would be exerting an "exchange demand" for money, even though this person does not intend to use the acquired gold as a medium of exchange.

2. In Keynes's view, the demand for money is a downward sloping function of the *nominal interest rate*, not the PPM. The idea is that the opportunity cost of holding cash (as opposed to investing the money in a bond, for example) rises with the nominal interest rate: At 10 percent holding a $10 bill means forfeiting $1 in future cash, whereas at 20 percent the decision costs $2 in forgone future money. Austrians reject this explanation because (1) the (pure) interest rate is determined by time preferences and (2) the true opportunity cost of holding money is not simply (the value of) a bond but (the value of) *all* other goods and services that could have been purchased with the cash.

3. The *reductio ad absurdum* on p. 839 may have lost the reader. Rothbard arrives at the middle fraction (which has "(hats) (pounds of sugar)" in the denominator) by adding the two fractions at the top of the page. But the reader must recall from algebra that in order to add two fractions, a common denominator is

Chapter 11: Money and Its Purchasing Power 151

necessary; Rothbard achieves it here by multiplying the left fraction by [(hats) / (hats)] and the right fraction by [(pounds of sugar) / (pounds of sugar)].

152   *Study Guide to Man, Economy, and State with Power and Market*

Study Questions

1. Why does Rothbard say that the exchange demand curves for money will tend to be perfectly inelastic? (p. 757)

2. Why is each of the components of the total demand curve for money downward sloping? (pp. 757–60)

3. The total demand for money is the summation of the (pre-income) exchange demand and the (post-income) reservation demand (pp. 756–61). Suppose a man sells a car for 10 ounces of gold, and then decides to hold this 10 ounces of money in his cash balance. Do his actions count as the demand for *20* ounces of gold?

4. Why does Rothbard depict the supply of money as a vertical line? (p. 763) As the PPM of money rises, wouldn't that induce people to mine more gold, etc.? Is Rothbard saying that the supply of money, unlike other goods, isn't upward sloping?

5. Rothbard says that "the 'price' of money is precisely the variable on which the demand schedule depends" (p. 765). Isn't this true of all commodities?

6. Is speculation in money simply a matter of "self-fulfilling prophecies"? (pp. 769–71)

Chapter 11: Money and Its Purchasing Power 153

7. When the demand for money changes, this alters the PPM and restores equilibrium. But does this translate into anything "real"? For example, if everyone doubles his or her cash balance, has anything really changed? If not, what purpose does it serve besides accommodating everyone's arbitrary whims?

8. In criticizing Keynes, Rothbard argues that, "Speculation . . . disappears in the ERE, and hence no fundamental causal theory can be based upon it" (p. 789). Does this argument eliminate Rothbard's ability to explain the earnings of stockbrokers or advertising executives?

9. What is the likely secular trend for the four determinants of the PPM in a progressing economy? (p. 817)

10. What are the problems with index numbers to measure the PPM? (pp. 845–46)

CHAPTER 12

THE ECONOMICS OF VIOLENT INTERVENTION IN THE MARKET

Chapter Summary

In this chapter we analyze (using economic science) the effects of violations of property rights, and in particular the effects of State action, i.e., *institutionalized* and widespread violations.

Intervention is the intrusion of aggressive physical force into society. *Autistic* intervention occurs when the aggressor uses force on an individual such that no one else is affected. *Binary* intervention occurs when the aggressor establishes a hegemonic relationship between himself and the victim. *Triangular* intervention occurs when the aggressor uses force to alter the relations between a pair of subjects.

The free market maximizes *ex ante* utilities and has mechanisms to promote *ex post* fulfillment of these plans. In contrast, each act of government intervention always harms at least one party, and moreover suffers from indirect consequences that further distort the economy.

A *price control* involves the use of force to alter the terms on which individuals exchange goods or services. Maximum prices lead to *shortages*, i.e., situations where quantity demanded exceeds quantity supplied. (A prime example is the shortage of apartments due to rent control.) Minimum prices lead to *surpluses*, i.e., situations where quantity supplied exceeds quantity

155

demanded. (A prime example is the unemployment due to the minimum wage.)

Both taxation and government spending distort the economy; the former drains resources away from the private sector while the latter distorts resource allocation away from what it otherwise would have been. There can be no such thing as a neutral tax, because taxation is coercive and thus differs fundamentally from a voluntary price. A so-called flat tax is not the equivalent of a price, because in the market rich customers do not pay in proportion to their income. A head tax would be closer, but it too is coercive; some taxpayers would be forced to fund certain government activities that they abhor.

It is a myth that taxes on a firm can be "passed on" to customers. If firms could really do this—i.e., raise prices to generate extra revenues to offset a new tax—then why didn't the firms do it before? It is true that a tax will eventually raise prices paid by consumers, but this is achieved by lowering profitability and hence supply, which *then* raises the equilibrium price.

Economists often try to gauge the "productive contribution" of government activities by the size of its expenditures. Yet this is directly opposite from the market approach, where value is gauged by how much customers spend *on* products, not by how much the business itself spends in making them!

In a credit expansion the government artificially lowers the interest rate, thereby spurring investment in higher stages of production. There is a temporary "boom" period of illusory prosperity. With no genuine increase in saving, the capital structure becomes unbalanced and eventually entrepreneurs realize that their plans cannot be fulfilled. The "bust" ensues when businesses discontinue the unprofitable lines and resources must be reallocated to their proper uses.

Chapter 12: The Economics of Violent Intervention in the Market **157**

Chapter Outline

1. Introduction

The bulk of the book has concentrated on the free society, in which everyone respects property rights. In this chapter we analyze (using economic science) the effects of violations of property rights, and in particular the effects of State action, i.e., *institutionalized* and widespread violations. Note that economics does not "assume" *laissez-faire* at any point, but instead objectively demonstrates the outcomes of both free and coercive institutions.

2. A Typology of Intervention

Intervention is the intrusion of aggressive physical force into society. The economic analysis of "private" coercion is the same as government coercion, but we focus on the latter because of its greater prevalence and number of apologists. *Autistic* intervention occurs when the aggressor uses force on an individual such that no one else is affected. *Binary* intervention occurs when the aggressor establishes a hegemonic relationship between himself and the victim. *Triangular* intervention occurs when the aggressor uses force to alter the relations between a pair of subjects.

3. Direct Effects of Intervention on Utility

In a free market, people only participate in an exchange if they believe they will benefit; thus the market "maximizes" *ex ante* utility of everyone in society. Any intervention, in contrast, increases the utility of the aggressor and necessarily reduces the utility of the affected subjects.

158   *Study Guide to Man, Economy, and State with Power and Market*

4. Utility *Ex Post*: Free Market and Government

People always *expect* to benefit from voluntary exchanges, and in practice they usually *will* do so. In particular, inept businesses soon go bankrupt while entrepreneurs who make good forecasts earn profits. In contrast, in the government sector there are no mechanisms to minimize error. When a government policy fails in its stated objectives, the politicians do not necessarily suffer and the voters may not be sophisticated enough to perceive the true causes of the failure. (A good summary is at the bottom of p. 891.)

5. Triangular Intervention: Price Control

A *price control* involves the use of force to alter the terms on which individuals exchange goods or services. When the government sets a maximum price (or price ceiling), it threatens force against anyone caught charging a price above a specific amount. Maximum prices lead to *shortages*, i.e., situations where quantity demanded exceeds quantity supplied. (A prime example is the shortage of apartments due to rent control.) When the government sets a minimum price (or price floor), it makes it illegal to pay below a certain price. Minimum prices lead to *surpluses*, i.e., situations where quantity supplied exceeds quantity demanded. (A prime example is the unemployment due to the minimum wage.)

6. Triangular Intervention: Product Control

Product control regulates the product itself, or the people involved in the exchange. (In contrast price control regulates only the terms of trade.)

Chapter 12: The Economics of Violent Intervention in the Market   *159*

7. Binary Intervention: The Government Budget

When analyzing the effects of government taxation and spending, we need to use both a partial and general equilibrium approach (p. 910); a tax will (a) make the taxed item less attractive and (b) make the consumers poorer and so affect *other* markets too. Both taxation and government spending distort the economy; the former drains resources away from the private sector while the latter distorts resource allocation away from what it otherwise would have been.

8. Binary Intervention: Taxation

A. Income Taxation

Taxation penalizes production; it shifts resources from taxpayers to tax-consumers. Just as a parasite must take care not to kill its host, there is an upper limit on taxation. Even if formally neutral with regard to consumption and saving, the income tax tends to raise time preferences by reducing everyone's level of (lifetime) income.

B. Attempts at Neutral Taxation

Rothbard defines a *neutral* tax as "a tax which would affect the income pattern, and all other aspects of the economy, in the same way as if the tax were really a free-market price." There can be no such thing, because taxation is coercive and thus differs fundamentally from a voluntary price. A so-called flat tax is not the equivalent of a price, because in the market rich customers do not pay in proportion to their income. A head tax would be better (in this respect), but it too is coercive; some taxpayers would be forced to fund certain government activities that they abhor.

C. Shifting and Incidence: A Tax on an Industry

It is a myth (in both mainstream economics and the public at large) that taxes on a firm can be "passed on" to customers. If firms could really do this—i.e., raise prices to generate extra revenues to offset a new tax—then why didn't the firms do it before? It is true that a tax will eventually raise prices paid by consumers, but this is achieved by lowering profitability and hence supply, which *then* raises the equilibrium price.

D. Shifting and Incidence: A General Sales Tax

Even in the "obvious" case of a general sales tax, it is simply not true that businesses can pass on price hikes to customers. What happens instead is that the tax is shifted *backward* to the imputed DMVPs of the factors of production. Thus a firm reacts to a new tax *not* by raising its prices to customers, but by lowering its payments to factor owners.

E. A Tax on Land Values

Many analysts think that taxes on land do not distort, since (unlike other resources) land cannot shift out of a taxed industry. This is not true, because land owners provide a definite service by discovering and allocating land to the highest bidders. If the government imposed a 100 percent tax on ground rents, it is true that the real estate would not physically disappear. But the affected owners would certainly stop advertising the parcels in the hopes of finding higher bidders, and no one would try to find new plots of land.

Chapter 12: The Economics of Violent Intervention in the Market   *161*

F.   Taxing "Excess Purchasing Power"

Keynesians suggest taxation as a remedy for price inflation, by "sopping up" excess purchasing power. This suggestion has several flaws: Why are higher prices considered more burdensome than higher taxes? Also, why would the government's action reduce aggregate demand, since the government spends its tax revenues anyway? It also overlooks the fact that cause of price inflation is government inflation of the money supply.

9.   Binary Intervention: Government Expenditures

A.   The "Productive Contribution" of Government Spending

Economists often try to gauge the "productive contribution" of government activities by the size of its expenditures. Yet this is directly opposite from the market approach, where value is gauged by how much customers spend *on* products, not by how much the business itself spends in making them! So-called government "investment" is misnamed because there is no reason to believe such projects will serve the future consumption desires of consumers.

B.   Subsidies and Transfer Payments

Subsidies distort resource allocation relative to the free market outcome. It is particularly ironic when the government subsidizes activities that it (allegedly) wishes to minimize, such as poor relief.

C. Resource-Using Activities

Beyond its depletion of scarce resources that consumers would have preferred in other lines, government provision of goods and services is deficient because it often charges artificially low prices. For example the chronic water and electricity shortages in summer months, as well as everyday traffic jams, are due to below-equilibrium prices for these crucial goods.

D. The Fallacy of Government on a "Business Basis"

Government can never be run "as a business" because its revenues are obtained through coercion. Moreover, its enterprises often enjoy monopoly privileges.

E. Centers of Calculational Chaos

Even small-scale government enterprises are subject to Mises's critique of socialism. By severing the link between customer and revenue, government officials have no feedback mechanism and cannot decide, even *ex post*, if they are performing properly.

F. Conflict and the Command Posts

Government enterprises necessarily cause conflict. For example, consider the controversies over religion in government schools. By its very nature, the government acts on behalf of "society" and thus the lack of unanimity on a given issue will lead to strife.

G. The Fallacies of "Public" Ownership

Government enterprises are not "public" despite the common terminology. Citizens can test this theory by trying to exercise control over, or sell their shares in, "public" schools or "public" parks.

H. Social Security

Funds taken as "premiums" for social security schemes are not in fact invested, but instead are spent on immediate consumption by the government. Such schemes are not true insurance.

I. Socialism and Central Planning

The extent of socialism is overestimated in formally socialist countries such as the Soviet Union because of black markets and foreign prices for capital goods, while it is underestimated in formally capitalist countries such as the United States because of government lending to business. In the present analysis, a centrally planned economy can be viewed as a centrally *prohibited* economy.

10. Growth, Affluence, and Government

A. The Problem of Growth

Government efforts to stimulate "growth" lower utility because they force people to shift consumption from present to future beyond what their personal time preferences dictate. The Austrian understanding of the heterogeneous capital structure also shows the danger of arbitrary government "investment" in particular capital goods.

B. Professor Galbraith and the Sin of Affluence

In the early twentieth century capitalism allegedly provided too few goods, while the more modern objection is that it provides superfluous goods (at the expense of the "public sector"). If, as Galbraith claims, businesses can simply create wants through seductive advertising, why do they spend so much money conducting research on consumer tastes?

11. Binary Intervention: Inflation and Business Cycles

A. Inflation and Credit Expansion

Inflation is any artificial increase in the money supply. *Credit expansion* is a particular type of inflation where the new money enters the economy through the credit market. All inflation raises prices and distorts the market, but credit expansions are particularly pernicious as they cause the boom-bust cycle.

B. Credit Expansion and the Business Cycle

In a credit expansion the government artificially lowers the interest rate, thereby spurring investment in higher stages of production. There is a temporary "boom" period of illusory prosperity. But unlike a genuine expansion spurred by actual saving, in the case of credit expansion the capital structure becomes unbalanced and eventually entrepreneurs realize that their plans cannot be fulfilled. The "bust" ensues when businesses discontinue the unprofitable lines and resources must be reallocated to their proper uses.

C. Secondary Developments of the Business Cycle

The demand for money may be affected during the course of the business cycle, and this can make the adjustment process more difficult.

D. The Limits of Credit Expansion

Under a commodity standard, credit expansion is naturally limited by the need for redeemability. Even under a fiat standard, individual banks always face the possibility of a run. However, central banking greatly expands the scope for credit expansion.

E. The Government as Promoter of Credit Expansion

The government promotes credit expansion by weakening the above checks. For example, government guarantees of bank deposits lowers the likelihood of runs, and central banking allows a uniform credit expansion on the part of all member banks.

F. The Ultimate Limit: The Runaway Boom

In the face of hyperinflation, the public's demand for the fiat money drops precipitously, causing prices to rise even more than one would expect from the increases in supply. In extreme cases the currency will be abandoned altogether.

G. Inflation and Compensatory Fiscal Policy

The various government programs to "fight inflation" are absurd, since (price) inflation is caused by the government's expansion of the money supply.

166   Study Guide to Man, Economy, and State with Power and Market

12. Conclusion: The Free Market and Coercion

Contrary to popular opinion, the free market is not chaotic and harmful, but rather results in the best possible achievement of orderly commerce and psychic utilities for all members of society. In contrast, each act of government intervention always harms at least one party, and moreover suffers from indirect consequences that further distort the economy.

APPENDIX A:
Government Borrowing

Government borrowing is not inflationary *per se*; it merely diverts spending from private capital goods to projects favored by the government. However, to the extent that government borrowing is financed through credit expansion, inflation is a common side effect. Government borrowing is harmful because it siphons funds that would otherwise have gone into private investment.

APPENDIX B:
"Collective Goods" and "External Benefits": Two Arguments for Government Activity

Mainstream economics justifies government measures in the case of "public goods," which are those goods that cannot be excluded from nonpayers, and which can confer benefits on additional users without diminishing their usefulness to others. Prototypical examples of public goods are national defense and lighthouses. This theory is open to severe criticism, because many so-called public goods (national defense, roads) do not actually fit the criteria. In any event, even if such a public good exists, it does not follow that *government* must provide it.

Another popular justification concerns positive (negative) "externalities," where the market actions of two individuals

Chapter 12: The Economics of Violent Intervention in the Market   *167*

have spillover effects on third parties. On moral grounds, what is the problem if someone benefits from the voluntary actions of other people? From an economic standpoint, this approach too is flawed because it would include all sorts of things not normally considered a "market failure." For example, every time someone invests and increases the capital stock, this provides a positive externality on all workers. Should they therefore have some of their wages diverted to the investor?

168   Study Guide to Man, Economy, and State with Power and Market

Notable Contributions

• Rothbard's typology of intervention is original.

• Rothbard's analysis of the welfare effects of markets versus intervention (pp. 879–85) is based on his impressive work, "Toward a Reconstruction of Utility and Welfare Economics."

• Unlike many other free market economists, Rothbard (pp. 918–19 and pp. 962–73) does not exhibit an arbitrary "pro-growth" bias.

Chapter 12: The Economics of Violent Intervention in the Market   *169*

Technical Matters

1. In footnote 1 (p. 875), Rothbard is a bit loose and seems to imply that *praxeology* and *economics* are synonymous terms. Strictly speaking, economics is a subset of praxeology, which is the science of human action (p. 74). Even so, Rothbard's position *vis-à-vis* Edwin Cannan is still correct, for "violent interrelations"—particularly those created by the State—are certainly forms of action with catallactic effects.

2. In his discussion of monopoly grants (a form of product control) Rothbard apparently uses the same analysis that he earlier (chapter 10) took pains to destroy. However, as he points out (p. 903), the crucial distinction is that there really *is* a free market price and output to use as a benchmark against the outcome after the government privilege is granted. In contrast, on the free market there really is no such alternative "competitive" price and output with which to compare the "monopoly" outcome.

3. The discussion on pp. 905–06 highlights the fact that monopoly returns are capitalized into the value of assets such that the rate of return is the same as in any other line; that is, there are no lasting monopoly *profits*, even in this case where "monopoly price" is meaningful.

4. A mainstream economist might defend the orthodox treatment of tax incidence (pp. 927–34) by arguing that Rothbard is overlooking the changed incentives after the imposition of a tax. For example, it is true that producers could not raise prices before the tax, because if any did so, others would undercut him. But

after the tax this may no longer be true; all producers in the affected industry can raise prices because no one can operate profitably at the old price. (See question 9 below.)

5. In footnote 12 (p. 1003), Rothbard clarifies that his "natural rate" is the rate of return earned by businesses on the market, and is different from the loan rate of interest. (It is thus what Böhm-Bawerk means by the *originary* rate of interest.) In contrast, Knut Wicksell (as well as other Austrian expositions) uses the term "natural rate" to mean simply the free market rate, i.e., the rate that would prevail were it not for distortionary credit expansion.

Chapter 12: The Economics of Violent Intervention in the Market   *171*

Study Questions

1. Give an example of each of the three types of interventions (pp. 877–78).

2. Why does Rothbard say voluntary exchanges always increase utility? Doesn't the displaced businessman lose when his product is rendered obsolete by the competition? (pp. 882–83)

3. Can some private parties gain from a triangular intervention?

4. What is Gresham's Law? (p. 899)

5. Give some examples of product control (pp. 900–07).

6. If domestic competitors can eliminate the benefits from tariffs (p. 906), why do firms clamor for protectionist measures?

7. Summarize the objections to the "cost principle" in taxation (pp. 922–23).

8. Summarize the objections to the "benefit principle" in taxation (pp. 923–24).

9. Rothbard argues that a tax cannot be shifted forward because none of the determinants of price (supply and demand for money, etc.) has

changed (pp. 927–31). Rothbard instead claims that a tax can be shifted backward in the form of lower factor payments (p. 932). But couldn't someone argue that none of the determinants of wages, rents, etc. has changed? After all, if businesses can simply pass a tax backward, then why didn't they cut their employees' wages *before* the tax?

10. Summarize Rothbard's critique of Galbraith (pp. 973–88).

POWER AND MARKET
GOVERNMENT AND THE ECONOMY

CHAPTER 1

DEFENSE SERVICES ON THE FREE MARKET

Chapter Summary

Economists often talk of the "free market" without analyzing the nature of property rights, and in particular the legal system that would prevail in a truly free market society. Economists also typically assume that "the market" is a frail arrangement that crucially depends upon *government* provision of defense (broadly including military, police, and judicial services). However, if we are truly interested in studying the *free* market, we must suppose that even defense services are provided through voluntary exchange of justly derived property titles.

Two crucial aspects of the State are: (1) it derives funds through coercive taxation, and (2) it arrogates to itself a geographical monopoly.

One objection to market-based defense is that the State must initially define property rights, and *then* the market process can proceed. This is simply wrong, as legal scholars using their reason and voluntary persuasion can realize the objective properties of a free legal order. In particular, they would discover the necessity and justice of self-ownership and the homesteading principle.

A related objection is that defense is a necessary precondition of market activity, and hence the market cannot be trusted to provide it. Yet this argument would also prove that the State needs to provide food, clothing, or shelter.

175

A third objection is that there allegedly must be a court of final opinion. Yet the world itself has no such ultimate ruler; the minimal statists usually do not call for one world government.

A free market in defense would probably consist in protection agencies selling subscriptions and providing their services on call. Insurance companies would probably be involved, as they would stand to gain from limiting theft, property destruction, and violence to their clients. If two protection agencies had a dispute concerning interactions between their clients, they would almost certainly not resort to violence to settle the matter, as this would be expensive and would frighten off potential customers. Rather they would sign binding arbitration agreements and take their case to a third party, which would be chosen only because of past excellence and objectivity in such cases.

In a free society, the great majority of judges would unilaterally endorse the Law Code that enshrined the nonaggression axiom and spelled out its implications. The function of the judges would be to apply the Code to the specific cases brought before them *voluntarily* by disputants.

It is certainly possible that particular agencies might become criminal. The difference is that there would be no systematic *legalized* method of plunder in a libertarian society. Everyone would immediately recognize the criminal activities for what they were. In contrast, many subjects under States (especially democratic ones) view taxes as voluntary "contributions" that are agreed upon at the polls. Because of the excellent propaganda efforts of the intelligentsia, most people do not consider taxation as theft, or war as mass murder, or conscription as indentured servitude.

The notion of limited government is a contradiction. Once we abandon unbridled property rights, it is arbitrary to set limits on government.

Chapter 1: Defense Services on the Free Market 177

Notable Contributions

• Although Rothbard is not the first free-market economist, nor the first advocate of the stateless society, his work represented the most mature marriage of sound economics and antistatist political theory. The earliest representative of this view is Gustav de Molinari.

Technical Matters

1. The nonaggression axiom states that no individual may *initiate* the use of force. It is sometimes supplemented to explicitly prohibit the initiation of theft and fraud. Ultimately the axiom (upon which the libertarian Law Code would be built, according to Rothbard) means that the default position is a universal respect for everyone's just property rights. However, once someone violates those rights, at that point it is permissible to use force against the aggressor.

2. The nonaggression axiom immediately implies the "moderate" libertarian positions on drug prohibition, conscription, government schools, minimum wages, etc. Yet it also implies the "radical" abolition of all taxation and government monopoly of the courts.

3. A proponent of limited government might object to Rothbard's argument on the top of page 1055 along the following lines: "Yes, the 'worst' that could happen following an anarchist experiment is that the State would re-emerge, but it might be a far worse State than what we have now."

Chapter 1: Defense Services on the Free Market   *179*

Study Questions

1. What is the "insoluble contradiction" of those who believe the State must protect property rights? (pp. 1048–49)

2. Are there any historical precedents for Rothbard's vision of private law? (p. 1051)

3. Should an anarcho-capitalist be able to give a complete blueprint of a private defense industry? (p. 1051)

4. Would vigilantism be allowed in Rothbard's ideal society? (p. 1052, fn 3)

5. Wouldn't defendants be able to appeal their cases indefinitely? (p. 1053)

6. Would libertarians have to use force to enshrine the Law Code? (p. 1053, fn 4)

7. Do anarcho-capitalists naïvely assume that most people are basically good? (p. 1054)

8. Why might it be easier to contain rogue protection agencies under anarchy, rather than an expanding State under minarchy? (pp. 1054–55)

180   Study Guide to Man, Economy, and State with Power and Market

9. How do mainstream economists use the "collective goods" argument to justify the State? (p. 1055)

10. What is the "inner contradiction" of limited government? (p. 1056)

CHAPTER 2

FUNDAMENTALS OF INTERVENTION

Chapter Outline

1. Types of Intervention

Intervention is the intrusion of aggressive physical force into society. The economic analysis of "private" coercion is the same as government coercion, but we focus on the latter because of its greater prevalence and number of apologists. *Autistic* intervention occurs when the aggressor uses force on an individual such that no one else is affected. *Binary* intervention occurs when the aggressor establishes a hegemonic relationship between himself and the victim. *Triangular* intervention occurs when the aggressor uses force to alter the relations between a pair of subjects.

2. Direct Effects of Intervention on Utility

A. Intervention and Conflict

In a free market, people only participate in an exchange if they believe they will benefit; thus the market "maximizes" *ex ante* utility of everyone in society. Any intervention, in contrast, increases the utility of the aggressor and necessarily reduces the utility of the affected subjects.

181

B. Democracy and the Voluntary

It is wrong to view State action in a democratic government as "voluntary." At best, only the *majority* of voters achieve their ends via democracy. Moreover, even the winning voters may have picked the "lesser of two evils." Note that no one uses such language in describing market purchases.

C. Utility and Resistance to Invasion

It is true that private defense agencies lower the utility experienced by an aggressor. However, the aggressor was himself interfering with the voluntary market by initiating force. It is still true that the free market (even with force-wielding defense agencies) maximizes utility for all of the noncriminals.

D. The Argument From Envy

One could object that the market does *not* necessarily maximize utility, because of envy. For example, it may not be true that a voluntary exchange of money for labor makes the two people better off (at least in their own *ex ante* estimation) and does nothing else; perhaps a third party is disappointed that *he* was not hired for the job. From a praxeological viewpoint, however, all we can analyze is concrete *action*; we cannot speculate on someone's inner feelings. Even if someone publishes pamphlets denouncing the sale of tobacco, there is no ironclad proof that this person is not committing a practical joke.

E. Utility *Ex Post*

People always *expect* to benefit from voluntary exchanges, and in practice they usually *will* do so. In

Chapter 2: Fundamentals of Intervention 183

particular, inept businesses soon go bankrupt while entrepreneurs who make good forecasts earn profits. In contrast, in the government sector there are no mechanisms to minimize error. When a government policy fails in its stated objectives, the politicians do not necessarily suffer and the voters may not be sophisticated enough to perceive the true causes of the failure. It is ironic that advocates of democracy do not trust citizens to make personal decisions but *do* trust them to vote for wise politicians.

184   *Study Guide to Man, Economy, and State with Power and Market*

Notable Contributions

• Rothbard's typology of intervention is original. (Much of the analysis in *Power and Market* was summarized in Chapter 12 of *Man, Economy, and State* when Rothbard learned that he would have to split up the volumes.)

Chapter 2: Fundamentals of Intervention

Technical Matters

1. Some have objected to Rothbard's claim that the free market maximizes utility because protection agencies necessarily make criminals less happy through their protection of clients. To elaborate on Rothbard's defense (p. 1068), consider that once someone initiates aggression, it is *impossible* to achieve Pareto improvements (relative to the starting point of the analysis). If just one person is willing to violate property rights, we can no longer achieve unanimity in value judgments regarding the desirability of particular actions, and economic analysis alone can say no more. However, as Rothbard points out, there is still a presumption in favor of *private* defense agencies, because in principle they could exist in a crime-free world, where social utility *would* be maximized. (This is because the defense agencies would have contractual, voluntary arrangements with their customers, and thus we would still have an unblemished free market.) In contrast, under a State even if all of the citizens respected property rights, the State itself would still be initiating aggression and hence the economist could make no welfare claims.

2. Some economists have criticized Rothbard's defense of his utility maximization claim from the "envy" objection (pp. 1068–69). For example, Bryan Caplan has argued that, were we to follow Rothbard's logic, we *also* could not conclude that people signing a contract really wanted to cement a deal; perhaps the signers were merely practicing penmanship. And yet this is no contradiction on the part of Rothbard: as praxeologists, we *can't* say that someone signing a

contract agrees to the terms it spells out. After all, the person could be illiterate, force could have been threatened earlier, etc. (It is not *praxeology* that spells out the conditions for a legally enforceable contract.) What praxeology *can* say is that, at the moment of choice, the person thought that signing the contract would yield more utility than any rival course of action. Remember, the reason the praxeologist can also comment on coercive outcomes is that they necessarily differ from voluntary scenarios. (If they didn't, then the aggressor wouldn't bother threatening force.) *That* is why praxeologists conclude that voluntary actions increase utility while coerced ones harm at least one party. If at gunpoint two people agree to an exchange, then the praxeologist has no "ironclad proof" that they really possessed a reverse valuation for the items; Rothbard is thus not being pedantic just to rescue his welfare theory.

Chapter 2: Fundamentals of Intervention   *187*

Study Questions

1. What were Oppenheimer's two means of satisfying wants? (pp. 1057–58)

2. Why doesn't it matter whether an intervention is "legal" or not? (p. 1057)

3. On which type of intervention do most political economists focus? (pp. 1059–60)

4. What is the distinction between classes and castes? (p. 1062, fn 5)

5. Rothbard characterizes the State as inherently coercive, and yet he agrees with Hume that *all* governments rest on the consent of the governed (p. 1066, fn 9). Is this a contradiction?

6. Won't ignorant consumers make poor choices on the market? (p. 1070)

7. Doesn't advertising weaken the alleged virtues of the free market? (p. 1071)

8. Can't voters choose expert politicians in a responsible manner? (pp. 1071–72)

9. Why is there no concrete test of success in government? (p. 1072)

10. Why might intervention be undesirable *ex post* even in the eyes of its initial supporters? (p. 1073)

CHAPTER 3

TRIANGULAR INTERVENTION

Chapter Summary

Price control occurs when the intervener attempts to influence the terms on which products or services exchange. (In contrast *product control* is a coercive influence on the product or service itself, including the individuals who sell it.) A price control is *ineffective* if its penalties do not apply because the market price falls within the legally permissible range. The rest of the analysis assumes an effective price control.

A *maximum* price control occurs when the intervener threatens violence against anyone caught selling a good above a particular price. The immediate effect is a *shortage*. "Nonprice rationing" then comes into play, including queues, favoritism for certain customers, and discrimination against unpopular groups.

A *minimum* price control threatens violence to prevent sales of a good or service below a particular price. This leads to a *surplus*. An example is the mass unemployment caused by minimum wage laws.

Outright *prohibition* leads to black markets as suppliers sell the product outside legal channels. The reduced supply leads to higher prices, but also to an inferior product as the sellers cannot resort to economies of scale and name-brand advertising.

By prohibiting sale of a good or service except for a privileged group, the government confers an artificial monopoly (or

189

190   *Study Guide to Man, Economy, and State with Power and Market*

oligopoly) grant. All of the alleged effects of free market cartels and monopolies *do* apply to *government* cartels and monopolies. Following are examples of typical monopoly grants:

Compulsory cartels occur when the government forces firms in an industry to restrict output. This helps inefficient firms and hurts consumers.

Licensing is a threat of violence that limits the permissible producers to particular groups (those who have obtained the license). The ostensible purpose of most licensing is to ensure quality and safety for consumers. Even so, the intervener necessarily eliminates the option of lower-quality but cheaper services. On the free market, sellers of adulterated products could be prosecuted for fraud and/or injuring the buyer's body.

A *tariff* is a tax placed on imports in a particular industry. It directly injures domestic consumers and foreign producers, and it indirectly injures domestic exporters in other industries. *Immigration restrictions* confer a restrictionist wage to the domestic laborers, raise prices to consumers, and distort the location of workers and capital.

Child labor laws raise wages for adult workers and reduce total output. Compulsory school attendance lowers utility even more than a mere prohibition on work.

Conscription reduces the supply of able-bodied adult laborers, distorting production and raising wages.

Government unemployment benefits slow the transferral of displaced workers to new jobs, and help mask the harmful effects of unionism and other restrictionist policies.

Antitrust laws stifle efficient mergers and penalize those firms that gain market share by satisfying customers. *Conservation laws* defy the time preference schedules of individuals and confer gains to particular factor owners. On a free market, owners tend to maximize the present discounted value of their assets.

Chapter 3: Triangular Intervention 191

Chapter Outline

1. Price Control

Price control occurs when the intervener attempts to influence the terms on which products or services exchange. (In contrast *product control* is a coercive influence on the product or service itself, including the individuals who sell it.) A price control is *ineffective* if its penalties do not apply because the market price falls within the legally permissible range. The rest of the analysis assumes an effective price control.

A *maximum* price control occurs when the intervener threatens violence against anyone caught selling a good above a particular price. The immediate effect is a *shortage*, when the quantity demanded exceeds the quantity supplied. "Nonprice rationing" then comes into play, including queues, favoritism for certain customers, and discrimination against unpopular groups. Sellers may also reduce the quality of the product, e.g., landlords who do not maintain a building because of rent controls.

A *minimum* price control threatens violence to prevent sales of a good or service below a particular price. This leads to a *surplus*, when the quantity supplied exceeds the quantity demanded. An example is the mass unemployment caused by minimum wage laws.

2. Product Control: Prohibition

Prohibition leads to black markets as suppliers sell the product outside legal channels. The reduced supply leads to higher prices, but also to an inferior product as the sellers cannot resort to economies of scale and name-brand advertising.

Partial prohibitions involve prohibitions after a certain point; examples include rationing systems and maximum-hour laws.

3. Product Control: Grant of Monopolistic Privilege

By prohibiting sale of a good or service except for a privileged group, the government confers an artificial monopoly (or oligopoly) grant. All of the alleged effects of free market cartels and monopolies (that are in truth illusory) *do* apply to *government* cartels and monopolies.

A. Compulsory Cartels

In order to lower the embarrassing gluts of minimum price controls, governments will often impose maximum production quotas on an industry, i.e., will force all of the relevant firms to join a cartel. Inefficient producers benefit at the expense of their efficient competitors.

B. Licenses

A popular form of monopolistic grant is the *license*, in which the government threatens violence against any producer who does not first obtain the license.

C. Standards of Quality and Safety

The ostensible purpose of most licensing is to ensure quality and safety for consumers. Even so, the intervener necessarily eliminates the option of lower-quality but cheaper services. Moreover, such regulation locks in particular standards and slows improvements. On the free market, sellers of adulterated products could be prosecuted for fraud and/or injuring the buyer's body.

Chapter 3: Triangular Intervention   *193*

D. Tariffs

A tariff is a tax placed on imports from foreign producers in a particular industry, designed to "protect" the domestic suppliers. It directly injures domestic consumers (by raising prices) and foreign producers, and it indirectly injures domestic exporters in other industries by restricting the sales of foreigners. (A country ultimately pays for its imports with exports, and thus to restrict another country's exports will reduce its demand for one's own exported products.)

E. Immigration Restrictions

Restrictions on foreign workers confer a restrictionist wage to the domestic laborers. Such restrictions distort the location of workers and capital (investors will export more capital because of the artificially high domestic wages) and raise prices for consumers.

F. Child Labor Laws

Child labor laws raise wages for adult workers and reduce total output. Compulsory school attendance is an even worse means of eliminating child labor, as it not only prevents children from working but also compels them to participate in a specific alternate activity.

G. Conscription

The draft reduces the supply of able-bodied adult laborers, distorting production and raising wages. It also allows the government to field an army for a lower monetary expenditure than would be necessary to raise a volunteer army of comparable size.

H. Minimum Wage Laws and Compulsory Unionism

To the extent that government measures (such as the Wagner-Taft-Hartley Act) allow unions greater scope to coercively restrict the labor supply, they raise wages for the privileged workers and reduce them for the non-members.

I. Subsidies to Unemployment

Government unemployment benefits slow the transferal of displaced workers to new jobs, and help mask the harmful effects of unionism and other restrictionist policies.

J. Penalties on Market Forms

Arbitrary penalties on specific organizations harm efficient producers. Examples include taxes on chain stores, laws limiting hours of business operation, outlawing of pushcart peddlers, and corporate income taxes.

K. Antitrust Laws

As the only sensible criterion of trust or monopoly is a legal privilege conferred by government, the antitrust laws are necessarily vague. They stifle efficient mergers and penalize those firms that gain market share by satisfying customers.

L. Outlawing Basing-Point Pricing

On the free market, one price will prevail *at the point of consumption*, but producers may charge different prices

Chapter 3: Triangular Intervention

"at the mill" (because of different costs of transportation) in order to remain competitive. Government rulings that this constitutes "price-fixing" distort the location of production centers and thus hamper efficiency.

M. Conservation Laws

Government measures designed to preserve nonrenewable resources defy the time preference schedules of individuals and confer gains to particular factor owners.

Whenever a unit of such a resource is consumed, it will be in the "present." Why then should future generations receive special consideration, especially since they will be wealthier than the present generation? Conservation laws do not provide more for the future, but at best only provide more *natural* resources at the expense of capital goods.

Private owners tend to maximize the present discounted value of their assets. Conservation laws would only make sense if government bureaucrats were better at forecasting future uses for resources than businesspeople were.

N. Patents

A *patent* is a monopoly privilege granted to first discoverers of certain inventions. Far from being a legitimate form of property right, a patent is a restriction on the ability of others to use their property. The utilitarian argument for patents—that they are necessary to stimulate the "proper" amount of research and development—relies on an arbitrary value judgment that the free market level of research would be "too low." Patents do not in fact encourage innovation *per se*, but rather distort the relative amounts of innovation in patentable and non-patentable fields.

O. Franchises and "Public Utilities"

Franchises (in this context) are grants to use government streets. If they are restrictive, they are grants of monopoly. However, the issue is complicated by the fact that governments (illegitimately) own the streets and therefore must make some decision over usage.

P. The Right of Eminent Domain

The right of eminent domain allows a privileged group to compel the sale of property (generally land). For example, a railroad may be allowed to force homeowners to sell their property located in the path of a proposed new line. Eminent domain is of course a brazen violation of property rights that results in distortions in relative levels of investment.

Q. Bribery of Government Officials

Praxeologically, bribery is identical to sale of a government license to engage in a (nominally illegal) act. A *defensive* bribe mitigates the harm of government restrictions, while an *invasive* bribe is a further step away from the free market.

R. Policy Toward Monopoly

All true monopolies are conferred by government privilege and can be eliminated quite easily. Limited liability corporations do *not* enjoy special government privileges; on the free market investors could form such a

Chapter 3: Triangular Intervention 197

company and any employee or customer would deal with them at his or her own risk.

APPENDIX A:
On Private Coinage

The typical justification for government control of the mint is that reliable standards are necessary in money. This argument ignores the abysmal record of government debasement, and it also proves far too much: Exact standards are necessary for machine-tools, yet this does not prove the need for a nationalization of this industry. On the free market private firms could certify coins and stamp them with a name brand.

APPENDIX B:
Coercion and *Lebensraum*

Restrictions on trade and immigration lead to hostility between nations. If a given country is truly "overpopulated," it is only because of government restrictions on immigration by its neighbors.

Notable Contributions

• Rothbard continues with his exhaustive classification of intervention. In this chapter he takes his original concept of a "triangular intervention" and analyzes typical government measures from this perspective.

• Rothbard's pioneering work in monopoly theory provides the background for his treatment of government "antimonopoly" policy.

Chapter 3: Triangular Intervention   *199*

Technical Matters

1. In chapter 10 of *Man, Economy, and State*, Rothbard exploded the mainstream theory of monopoly price. In particular, Rothbard claimed that this theory rested upon an alleged dichotomy between the "competitive" price and the "monopoly" price. Yet on a free market, there is only the free market price; there is no basis upon which one could criticize the outcome of voluntary exchanges even when there are only one or a few sellers. In contrast, when the *government* establishes a cartel or monopoly, then we *do* have a sensible benchmark, namely the "free market" price and level of output.

2. A government license on a business always hampers the satisfaction of the consumers, but it may not necessarily confer a monopoly price; depending on the demand in the industry, the licensed producers may find it most profitable to expand production to offset the elimination of unlicensed producers. In contrast, licensing of labor *always* raises wage rates; the licensed workers (generally) cannot sell more labor hours to completely offset the elimination of the unlicensed workers (p. 1096).

Study Questions

1. Why does Rothbard call the black market "the" market? (p. 1079)

2. What is Rothbard's suggested restatement of Gresham's Law? (pp. 1080–81)

3. What caused the "dollar shortage" in Europe after World War II? (p. 1082)

4. Why are legal tender laws classified as price controls? (p. 1083)

5. How do usury laws hurt their intended beneficiaries? (p. 1084)

6. Why does prohibition hurt both parties to an exchange, whereas price control arguably helps at least one party? (p. 1086)

7. If the owner of a building would be sent to jail for manslaughter, would auto producers (or owners) be jailed after every car accident in a free society? (p. 1099)

8. What is the fallacy of the infant industries justification for tariffs? (pp. 1105–07)

9. Why should the advocate of immigration controls also favor compulsory birth control? (p. 1111)

Chapter 3: Triangular Intervention   *201*

10. Does Rothbard think that children should work instead of going to school? (pp. 1111–12)

CHAPTER 4

BINARY INTERVENTION: TAXATION

Chapter Summary

Society is composed of taxpayers and tax consumers. The tax consumers benefit from taxation while the taxpayers foot the bill. All taxation distorts resource allocation and severs "distribution" from production. The *total level* of taxation is far more significant than the specific forms of the tax.

Tax *incidence* refers to the actual long-run burden of taxation, which may differ from the immediate target. *No tax can be shifted forward.* (If retailers had this power, why wait for the tax?) All sales taxes are ultimately *income* taxes.

An income tax reduces the utility of the taxpayers, and generally provides a disincentive to earn income. Income taxes may indirectly raise time preference rates by reducing overall income. It is no more odious to impair savings than consumption.

Taxes on wages cannot be shifted to the employer. Corporate taxes are examples of "double" taxation. This encourages stockholders to leave the net income as "undistributed" earnings and hence distorts the flow of funds. A capital gain is a form of income, just as other types of profit. If we desire the (unattainable) goal of uniform taxation, one would need to correct capital gains for inflation.

Proposals to directly tax consumption merely translate to an income tax. Such a tax does *not* favor savings, because the point

203

of savings is to consume in the future (when the tax will also operate).

In contrast to a tax on *current* savings, the charge of "double taxation" is coherent when it comes to taxes on accumulated capital. These destroy the inherited tools, equipment, etc. from the past, and thus a 20 percent tax on capital is far more destructive than a 20 percent tax on income.

The typical arguments against the progressive tax are that (1) it reduces the incentive to work, (2) it reduces savings, and (3) it is robbery of the rich by the poor. The first argument is correct, but this is also true of a proportional tax. The second argument is also correct, but those making it usually imply (with no justification) that it is somehow worse to reduce saving than to reduce consumption. The third argument is wrong: Under progressive taxation, the *government* robs both the rich and the poor.

The Georgist proposal to tax ground rent ignores the owners' role in allocating land to the most value-productive users. There would indeed be no incentive to charge rents *at all*; this would eliminate the Georgist tax base and cause severe distortions in the allocation of scarce land.

The only objectively "just price" is the market price. Economists have generally abandoned the medieval quest for the just price, yet they cling to the notion of a just tax.

It is impossible to tax everyone uniformly. First there is the distinction between taxpayers and tax consumers; since the latter pay *no taxes*, clearly "uniformity" is only possible if no one pays any taxes. Second, there is the problem of defining *income*. For example, should it include services in kind? Should it be calculated as a yearly average?

If each taxpayer were truly taxed according to how much he or she benefited from government services, then it would be pointless to provide the services in the first place. Moreover, all bureaucrats would have to work for free.

Chapter 4: Binary Intervention: Taxation   *205*

Chapter Outline

1. Introduction: Government Revenues and Expenditures

Government derives its revenue (income) from taxation and inflation. This chapter assumes that all revenue is spent.

2. The Burdens and Benefits of Taxation and Expenditures

Society is composed of taxpayers and tax consumers. The tax consumers (politicians, bureaucrats, and subsidized citizens) benefit from taxation while the taxpayers foot the bill, though the exact effects are difficult to trace. All government spending is *consumption* (not investment). All taxation distorts resource allocation and severs "distribution" from production (whereas there is no such distinction in a market). The *total level* of taxation is far more significant than the specific *forms* of the tax.

3. The Incidence and Effects of Taxation

Part I: Taxes on Incomes

A. The General Sales Tax and the Laws of Incidence

Tax *incidence* refers to the actual long-run burden of taxation, which may differ from the immediate target. Contrary to popular and even mainstream economics belief, *no tax can be shifted forward*. Even in the "obvious" case of a general sales tax, it is not true that the retailers can "pass on" the tax in the form of higher prices. (If they had this power, why wait for the tax?) They stay in business by shifting the tax *backward* to the factor owners. Thus all sales taxes are ultimately *income* taxes.

B. Partial Excise Taxes; Other Production Taxes

An excise tax distorts resource allocation (as all taxes do) by shifting demand from consumers to politicians, but also because it only applies to particular goods. Excise taxes too are ultimately taxes on income, not just consumption.

C. General Effects of Income Taxation

Because sales and other taxes are ultimately taxes on income, this section is not confined to the "official" income tax. An income tax naturally reduces the utility of the taxpayers, and generally provides a disincentive to earn income. (Even if someone ends up working *greater hours* to offset the tax, this still represents a loss of utility.) Income taxes may *indirectly* raise time preference rates by reducing overall income. They also encourage unofficial work, e.g., "do it yourself" projects, and hence impair the division of labor. Contrary to many "right wing" economists, it is no more odious to impair savings than consumption.

D. Particular Forms of Income Taxation

(1) Taxes on Wages

Taxes on wages cannot be shifted to the employer. In fact, the opposite is true. The employer contribution for Social Security is ultimately deducted from the employee's wage.

(2) Corporate Income Taxation

Corporate taxes are examples of "double" taxation. This encourages stockholders to leave

Chapter 4: Binary Intervention: Taxation 207

the net income as "undistributed" earnings and hence distorts the flow of funds.

(3) "Excess" Profit Taxation

This is a direct penalty on successful entrepreneurship.

(4) The Capital Gains Problem

A capital gain is a form of income, just as other types of profit. If we desire the (unattainable) goal of uniform taxation, one would need to correct capital gains for inflation.

(5) Is a Tax on Consumption Possible?

Proposals (such as Irving Fisher's) to directly tax consumption merely translate to an income tax (albeit at a lower rate). Such a tax does *not* favor savings, because the point of savings is to consume in the future (when the tax will also operate). (This conclusion only holds if we rule out dishoarding or dissaving.)

4. The Incidence and Effects of Taxation

Part II: Taxes on Accumulated Capital

In contrast to a tax on *current* savings, the charge of "double taxation" is coherent when it comes to taxes on accumulated capital. These destroy the inherited tools, equipment, etc. from the past, and thus a 20 percent tax on capital is far more destructive than a 20 percent tax on income.

A. Taxation on Gratuitous Transfers: Bequests and Gifts

Gifts are transfers, rather than payment for production. Consequently taxes on gifts are taxes on capital. These taxes weaken private charity and family ties.

B. Property Taxation

Property taxes must rely on assessed values which can't be known outside of market sales. They also penalize property under debt because of "double taxation." Taxes on rents are capitalized in the sale price of assets and do not fall on future buyers.

C. A Tax on Individual Wealth

Although no one proposes it, we can analyze the effects of a hypothetical tax on individual wealth. Like an income tax, it could not be shifted. Unlike a tax on property, it could not be capitalized and hence the market could not "contain" its harmful effects after the initial shock.

5. The Incidence and Effects of Taxation

Part III: The Progressive Tax

The typical arguments against the progressive tax are that (1) it reduces the incentive to work, (2) it reduces savings, and (3) it is robbery of the rich by the poor. The first argument is correct, but this is also true of a proportional tax. The second argument is also correct, but those making it usually imply (with no justification) that it is somehow worse to reduce saving than to reduce consumption. The third argument is wrong: Under

Chapter 4: Binary Intervention: Taxation

progressive taxation, the *government* robs both the rich and the poor.

6. The Incidence and Effects of Taxation

Part IV: The "Single Tax" on Ground Rent

The Georgist proposal to tax ground rent is severely flawed. The taxing agency must make estimates of ground rent, and moreover determine how much of gross rent is really the return to the land, and how much reflects interest and wages. (These returns are jumbled in the real world whenever original land has been augmented.) The Georgist theory ignores the role of time, and hence misunderstands cases of idle land with a positive capital value. If ground rents were fully taxed, then owners would cease performing their vital role of allocating land to the most value-productive users. There would indeed be no incentive to charge rents *at all*; this would eliminate the Georgist tax base and cause severe distortions in the allocation of scarce land.

7. Canons of "Justice" in Taxation

A. The Just Tax and the Just Price

The only objectively "just price" is the market price. Economists have generally abandoned the medieval quest for the just price, yet they cling to the notion of a just tax. Adam Smith advanced four criteria of justice in taxation that are analyzed below.

B. Costs of Collection, Convenience, and Certainty

It is not at all obvious that a given tax should be administered with the least possible cost; a costly tax may be implemented less vigorously. It is also possible that an *inconvenient* tax may be beneficial by encouraging the taxpayers to protest. It is also arguable that if a tax is *uncertain* that the taxpayer benefits, because now he or she has "wiggle room" when it comes to assessing total tax liability.

C. Distribution of the Tax Burden

There are various proposals for "justice" in distributing the tax burden:

(1) Uniformity of Treatment

(a) Equality before the law: tax exemption

Equality of treatment is not a virtue if the "treatment" is itself unjust! For example, if someone proposes to enslave others, it is much better that he ensnares only a few rather than enslaving everyone equally. Exemptions are not at all subsidies, because the government is not the rightful owner of one's money. They are not really "loopholes" but rather just the law.

(b) The impossibility of uniformity

It is impossible to tax everyone uniformly. First there is the distinction between taxpayers and tax consumers; since the latter pay no taxes, clearly "uniformity" is only possible if no one pays any taxes. Second, there is the problem of defining *income*. For example, should it include services in kind? Should it be calculated as a yearly average?

(2) The "Ability-to-Pay" Principle

(a) The ambiguity of the concept

There are many plausible approaches to defining one's "ability to pay" a tax; this underscores the arbitrariness of the concept.

(b) The justice of the standard

It is impossible to justify the "ability to pay" principle; it has been taken as self-evident. On the market, such a principle would lead to disaster.

(3) Sacrifice Theory

Some economists have attempted to justify progressive taxation on the basis of declining marginal utility of money, but this relies on nonsensical interpersonal utility comparisons.

(4) The Benefit Principle

Some economists conflate the benefit and cost principle when they justify proportional taxation on the grounds that the rich benefit more from government protection than the poor. Yet this assumes that the government somehow helped them earn their incomes. On its own terms, the benefit principle is nonsense: If each taxpayer were truly taxed according to how much he or she benefited from government services, then it would be pointless to provide the services in the first place. Moreover, all bureaucrats would have to work for free.

(5) The Equal Tax and the Cost Principle

In many respects a uniform head tax on all citizens would be more neutral than other proposals, but it too would require bureaucrats to work for free. It would deviate from a market price in that some people use more government services than others, yet would pay the same "price." The cost principle is flawed because government costs are higher than private analogs and there is no guarantee that a government agency's budget correlates to the benefits received by citizens.

(6) Taxation "For Revenue Only"

This slogan is silly since all taxes are "for revenue." The government can implement all sorts of "social engineering" through the *expenditure* side.

(7) The Neutral Tax: A Summary

The quest for a *neutral* tax, i.e., one that does not distort the outcomes that would occur in a free market, is hopeless.

D. Voluntary Contributions to Government

Even if taxpayers made voluntary contributions to pay for government activities, there would still be no

Chapter 4: Binary Intervention: Taxation   *213*

direct link between payment and service. Such a system would not be truly voluntary because of government prohibition on competitors. If competing legal and defense firms were permitted, then we would have a free market.

Notable Contributions

• As Rothbard notes (p. 1160), his analysis of tax incidence—and in particular the conclusion that taxes can't
be shifted forward—follows from the Austrian understanding of causality in market prices. Both the neoclassical and Austrian would agree that the equilibrium price of
a radio could be higher after the imposition of a tax on
sellers, and that (in a sense) consumers are bearing some
of the tax burden. However, Rothbard emphasizes that
the price rise is not "caused" by the tax, but rather the tax
puts marginal sellers out of business, and then the marginal utility of the smaller supply of radios allows sellers
to charge a higher price. The typical treatment of tax
incidence subtly relies on a cost theory of prices.

Chapter 4: Binary Intervention: Taxation 215

Technical Matters

1. The issue of "double taxation" can be confusing. Many economists argue that the income tax favors consumption and penalizes saving, because (say) if there is a ten percent income tax and Smith buys a savings bond, then Smith is first taxed on the income which he uses to buy the bond, and then Smith is taxed a second time when the bond matures and he is paid its face value. Reading Rothbard's critique (p. 1169) of Fisher and others—"There is therefore no reason here to say that an income tax especially penalizes savings-investment"—one might conclude that Rothbard *rejects* such an analysis. However, Rothbard later on (pp. 1169–70) does indeed admit that an income tax reduces the net interest rate earned on an investment, and to that extent it penalizes saving. The (suggested) resolution to this apparent contradiction is that Rothbard is taking Fisher et al. to be arguing (in our example) that a 10 percent income tax penalizes present consumption of $100 by $10, while it penalizes present *savings* of $100 by *more* than $10, since the $100 investment will yield more than $100 of income in the future. It is *this particular type of argument* that Rothbard rejects. (If this is indeed their argument, then a slightly different way to expose the fallacy is to point out that the "higher" absolute amount of taxation in the future must be converted to *present dollars* when deciding whether to consume or invest the $100 today. Thus the rate of return completely drops out of the analysis when assessing the tax's impact on present versus future consumption in this respect.)

2. In footnote 11 (p. 1157), Rothbard erroneously says that a tax on income causes a "rise in the opportunity cost of leisure," but it actually causes a *fall*, i.e., leisure becomes cheaper and thus people consume more of it. In footnote 36 (p. 1187), the final equation should be $C=R/(i+t)$. (In other words, Rothbard should have added parentheses for clarity.)

Chapter 4: Binary Intervention: Taxation

Study Questions

1. If tax consumers don't really pay taxes, is it also true that (say) Ford executives don't really pay for pickup trucks? (p. 1151, fn 3)

2. Why don't politicians keep all tax revenues for themselves? (p. 1152)

3. Rothbard says (p. 1158) that a sales tax cannot be shifted forward because businesses don't need a tax to raise prices (if that were really more profitable). But doesn't this also prove that a sales tax can't be shifted backward? (p. 1159) If businesses could get away with cutting wages, why wait for the sales tax?

4. If government officials happen to have lower time preferences than the society at large, couldn't an income tax increase savings? (pp. 1166–68)

5. Rothbard argues that taxes on *current* saving and investment are not really cases of "double taxation," whereas matters are different with taxes on capital accumulated in the past. Does this only apply to unanticipated, new taxes on capital, i.e., what if our forefathers knew their bequeathed capital stock would be taxed? Would this then constitute "single taxation"? (p. 1184)

6. Would a reduction in property taxes be a subsidy to landowners? (pp. 1188–89)

7. What is the *tax illusion* of the Chicago economists? (p. 1196)

8. What is the "land question," and how does the free market solve it? (p. 1209)

9. When are land speculators truly the bad guys? (pp. 1210–11)

10. Following the argument of footnote 58 (p. 1213), could someone legally get away with murder in a libertarian world, so long as he took care to wipe out his victim's entire family?

CHAPTER 5

BINARY INTERVENTION:
GOVERNMENT EXPENDITURES

Chapter Summary

There has been little economic *analysis* of government expenditure. Although in the real world the two are always mixed, we may conceptually distinguish between *pure transfers* and *resource-using* expenditures.

All subsidies transfer income from the efficient to the inefficient and distort resource allocation. They lower overall production by (1) diverting energies into "rent seeking" and (2) lowering the incentives to produce.

Government agents spend funds in order to achieve their ends, and hence all government spending is *consumption*, not investment. No government service can be "free" because of the scarce resources involved, but by charging low (or zero) prices, the government causes shortages and conflict. It is vain for the government to run an enterprise "on a business basis," for the government enterprise raises its funds through coercion.

Socialism refers to government ownership of the "means of production." The U.S. is more socialistic than generally believed, because of government loans (or guarantees) to business. The U.S.S.R. was less socialistic than generally believed because it relied on market prices from abroad and black markets internally.

Ownership is the ultimate control and direction of a resource. The public cannot "own" a park or a school building.

Even government officials do not truly own resources at State disposal, because they enjoy only temporary control. In contrast to popular belief, politicians are inherently shortsighted and tend to use resources too quickly. Private owners, on the other hand, can always sell their property for its capitalized value, and thus will exploit it at the optimal rate.

Democracy refers to majority rule, but in the "classical" sense it means majority decision on policies, whereas in the "modern" sense it usually means majority decision on rulers ("representatives") who then decide on actual policies.

The principle of democracy is riddled with contradictions. Can the people vote to *end* a democracy (either by moving to dictatorship or ushering in a totally free market)? "Democratic socialism" is infeasible, because the government ultimately decides on how many resources go to various propaganda efforts, and can determine the occupations of the opposition leaders.

There is also the more fundamental question: Why is democracy supposed to be so good? There are countless historical examples of the public making ignorant and evil decisions. It is also far from obvious that democracy is an effective means to check the growth of State power.

Simon Kuznets originally measured the size of government production by taxes paid, operating on the analogy with consumer expenditures for a private good or service. The problem is that taxpayers do not *voluntarily* give their funds for such "services." The Department of Commerce instead calculates on the basis of the total "cost" of a given program, and hence the bigger the government deficit, the more it is "serving" the community.

Chapter 5: Binary Intervention: Government Expenditures 221

Chapter Outline

There has been little economic *analysis* of government expenditure. Although in the real world the two are always mixed, we may conceptually distinguish between pure transfers and *resource-using* expenditures.

1. Government Subsidies: Transfer Payments

All subsidies transfer income from the efficient to the inefficient and distort resource allocation. They lower overall production by (1) diverting energies into "rent seeking" and (2) lowering the incentives to produce.

2. Resource-Using Activities: Government Ownership versus Private Ownership

Government agents spend funds in order to achieve their ends, and hence all government spending is *consumption*, not investment. No government service can be "free" because of the scarce resources involved, but by charging low (or zero) prices, the government causes shortages and conflict.

It is vain for the government to run an enterprise "on a business basis," for the government enterprise raises its funds through coercion. Not only does this distort the incentives, it also makes it impossible for the State personnel to serve the desires of their "customers." Even if a State enterprise allows competition, and buys factors and sells output in an open market, its initial capital was raised by coercion and hence gives it an unwarranted advantage. Finally, if someone *really* wants the enterprise to be run "on a business basis," then he should favor complete privatization!

222   *Study Guide to Man, Economy, and State with Power and Market*

3. Resource-Using Activities: Socialism

Socialism refers to government ownership of the "means of production." The particular form of government (democracy, monarchy, etc.) and the particular ideology (fascist, communist, etc.) are irrelevant to the *economic* analysis of socialism. The U.S. is more socialistic than generally believed, because of government loans (or guarantees) to business. The U.S.S.R. was less socialistic than generally believed because it relied on market prices from abroad and black markets internally.

4. The Myth of "Public" Ownership

Ownership is the ultimate control and direction of a resource. The public cannot "own" a park or a school building; the citizen who believes otherwise should try setting policies or selling his aliquot ownership share.

Even government officials do not truly own resources at State disposal, because they enjoy only temporary control. In contrast to popular belief, politicians are inherently short-sighted and tend to use resources too quickly. Private owners, on the other hand, can always sell their property for its capitalized value, and thus will exploit it at the optimal rate.

5. Democracy

Democracy refers to majority rule, but in the "classical" sense it means majority decision on policies, whereas in the "modern" sense it usually means majority decision on rulers ("representatives") who then decide on actual policies. Although in principle democratic governments can be more or less laissez-faire, economics does have something to say about institutional biases.

The principle of democracy is riddled with contradictions. Can the people vote to *end* a democracy (either by moving to

Chapter 5: Binary Intervention: Government Expenditures

dictatorship or ushering in a totally free market)? "Democratic socialism" is infeasible, because the government ultimately decides on how many resources go to various propaganda efforts, and can determine the occupations of the opposition leaders.

The implementation of democracy is also riddled with problems. In a representative government, the delimitation of voting districts is completely arbitrary. National government and democracy are likewise inconsistent, because the only nonarbitrary pool of voters is the world population.

Besides these practical questions, there is the more fundamental one: Why is democracy supposed to be so good? There are countless historical examples of the public making ignorant and evil decisions. It is also far from obvious that democracy is an effective means to check the growth of State power.

APPENDIX:
The Role of Government Expenditures in National Product Statistics

Simon Kuznets originally measured the size of government production by taxes paid, operating on the analogy with consumer expenditures for a private good or service. The problem is that taxpayers do not *voluntarily* give their funds for such "services." The Department of Commerce instead calculates on the basis of the total "cost" of a given program, and hence the bigger the government deficit, the more it is "serving" the community. For a more accurate approach, economists ought to first calculate Net National Product and then subtract either total government taxes or expenditures, *whichever is higher*.

224   *Study Guide to Man, Economy, and State with Power and Market*

Notable Contributions

• Rothbard's rejection of the Keynesian concept of government "investment" (p. 1259) relies on a praxeological understanding of means and ends.

• Rothbard advances many novel objections to democracy (pp. 1279–91), most of which would be dismissed as unworthy of response by "serious" scholars because they are so fundamental.

Chapter 5: Binary Intervention: Government Expenditures   *225*

Technical Matters

1. The "ballots instead of bullets" justification for democracy (p. 1287) was one held by Mises, and relies on the insight of David Hume that *all* governments ultimately rest on the consent of the governed. Since the majority will ultimately achieve its desired government through revolution if necessary, Mises argued that periodic elections are essential to preserve the peace. (There is thus no presumption here that the majority of voters are likely to make wise decisions.) Rothbard's somewhat facetious analysis (pp. 1287–91) is simply taking this justification at face value. In other words, Rothbard is questioning whether democratic elections really *do* give us "what would have happened anyway," without the need for bloodshed.

2. By saying that the Commerce Department uses the "cost" of a government program as a proxy for level of output, Rothbard simply means that they use *expenditure* (rather than Kuznet's *taxation*) as the measure. This too is vitiated because of the failure to link consumers with payment. On the market, a firm's expenditures on resources are *not* related to the satisfaction of consumers *if the firm is suffering a loss*.

Study Questions

1. If government relief encourages poverty, why wouldn't private charity do the same? (pp. 1257–58)

2. If a politician gives a subsidy to a firm as a means to achieve a consulting position in four years, would that be *investment* from a praxeological viewpoint? (p. 1259)

3. Why can't government enterprises use the rule of marginal cost pricing to guide their decisions? (p. 1267)

4. What are the "command posts" controlled by the State? (p. 1270)

5. There are many suggestions for how private owners could, say, maintain adequate stocks of fish in lakes. Why can't the government just take those ideas and implement them? (p. 1278)

6. Why is "direct democracy" once again feasible? (p. 1284)

7. Why does Rothbard argue that a consistent democrat should favor supremacy of the executive? (p. 1285)

8. Couldn't the defender of representative democracy claim that voters are ignorant on the issues but can choose wise leaders? (pp. 1285–86)

Chapter 5: Binary Intervention: Government Expenditures 227

9. Why can't government statistics test economic theory? (p. 1292)

10. Why does Rothbard include transfer payments in his deduction from NNP? (pp. 1294–95)

CHAPTER 6

ANTIMARKET ETHICS: A PRAXEOLOGICAL CRITIQUE

Chapter Summary

Praxeology is a value-free science; economics alone cannot imply value judgments. However, praxeology can demonstrate that certain ethical values either (1) rely on *false* propositions concerning cause and effect or (2) are *conceptually impossible* of fulfillment.

If we can demonstrate that X is an impossible and hence absurd goal, then it follows that any attempts to move *toward* X are likewise absurd, because the means derive their justification (value) from the sought end.

The advocate of laissez-faire does not assume that all people always act in their interest; it asserts rather "that everyone should have the right to be free to pursue his own interest as he deems best." Once one admits that consumers' preferences may be overridden due to immoral tastes, there is no limit to government control of "evil" or "dangerous" books, newspapers, etc. It is entirely useless to use force to (attempt to) achieve moral behavior, because without an uncoerced choice people cannot be moral.

Another straw man critique assumes that the market would work only if men were angels. On the contrary, regardless of one's views concerning human nature, the market—which penalizes evil and rewards good—is far preferable to the government,

229

which promotes those individuals most adept at wielding coercion.

Considering the diversity of human skills and their different locations in time and space, "equality" is an obviously nonsensical goal. Beyond that, it is not clear why intellectuals, who ostensibly favor the autonomy and full development of the individual, would at the same time champion equality.

The alleged tradeoff between freedom and security is a false one. The future is uncertain and hence absolute security is impossible. However, the free market provides security through savings, entrepreneurship, insurance, and charity.

It is a myth that medieval craftsmen and peasants were perfectly happy, until modern capitalism "alienated" them from their labor. The status society forced workers to remain in very specific occupations, regardless of aptitude or interest.

The market doesn't deal in "material" goods so much as *exchangeable* goods (and services). To the extent that the market provides ever greater quantities of exchangeable goods, it lowers their marginal utilities and hence raises the relative importance of *nonexchangeable* goods.

Many allege that the unregulated market would implement Social Darwinism in which the strong destroyed the weak. Yet this biological analogy overlooks the criterion of "fitness" in a marketplace: serving the wishes of the consumers.

References to "robber barons" and "economic royalists" are inappropriate. The market economy is a positive sum game, in which there is a harmony of interests. As man's power *over nature* grows, civilization develops. Yet a rise in one man's power *over another man* retards growth and represents a net loss.

It is pointless to argue that "human rights" should trump property rights, for *all* rights are ultimately property rights. Moreover, they are property rights *of humans*.

Chapter 6: Antimarket Ethics: A Praxeological Critique   *231*

Chapter Outline

1. Introduction: Praxeological Criticism of Ethics

Praxeology is a value-free science; economics alone cannot imply value judgments. However, praxeology can demonstrate that certain ethical values either (1) rely on false propositions concerning cause and effect or (2) are *conceptually impossible* of fulfillment. Thus praxeology cannot indicate the correct value judgments, but it *can* "veto" absurd ones.

If we can demonstrate that X is an impossible and hence absurd goal, then it follows that any attempts to move *toward* X are likewise absurd, because the means derive their justification (value) from the sought end.

2. Knowledge of Self-Interest: An Alleged Critical Assumption

The advocate of laissez-faire does not, contrary to popular belief, assume or require that all or even most people always act in their interest; it asserts rather "that everyone should have the right to be free to pursue his own interest as he deems best." The consumers are admittedly not experts in all fields, but they can always hire experts to advise them. And if they are too ignorant to do so successfully, how then can they vote for wise politicians to choose for them?

3. The Problem of Immoral Choices

Once one admits that consumers' preferences may be overridden due to immoral tastes, there is no limit to government control of "evil" or "dangerous" books, newspapers, etc. It is entirely useless to use force to (attempt to) achieve moral behavior, because without an uncoerced choice people cannot be moral.

4. The Morality of Human Nature

Another straw man critique assumes that the market would work only if men were angels. On the contrary, regardless of one's views concerning human nature, the market—which penalizes evil and rewards good—is far preferable to the government, which promotes those individuals most adept at wielding coercion.

5. The Impossibility of Equality

Considering the diversity of human skills and their different locations in time and space, "equality" is an obviously nonsensical goal. Beyond that, it is not clear why intellectuals, who ostensibly favor the autonomy and full development of the individual, would at the same time champion equality.

6. The Problem of Security

The alleged tradeoff between freedom and security is a false one. The future is uncertain and hence absolute security is impossible. However, the free market provides security through savings, entrepreneurship, insurance, and charity.

7. Alleged Joys of the Society of Status

It is a myth that medieval craftsmen and peasants were perfectly happy, until modern capitalism "alienated" them from their labor. The status society forced workers to remain in very specific occupations, regardless of aptitude or interest. In any event, a return to the institutions of the Middle Ages would require the starvation of a large portion of the world's present population.

8. Charity and Poverty

Before charity can occur, prior *production* is necessary. The unhampered market is far more productive than any rival system and hence can create the most goods for everyone. It is also not truly "charity" to take property and distribute it to others at gunpoint. The government has no interest in solving the problems of those who (allegedly) need its help, but prefers that they remain indefinitely dependent.

9. The Charge of "Selfish Materialism"

Another typical objection is that the market, though it may be very productive, causes people to focus on material ends, rather than spiritual concerns. This criticism relies on the empty notion of an "economic" end. Yet economy is simply the application of means to achieve desired ends; there are no separate "economic" ends to be contrasted with idealistic or spiritual ends.

Even if we believe people should adopt altruistic ends, it still does not follow that the market is objectionable. Indeed, someone who seeks maximum monetary income is precisely the person catering to the wishes of others (the consumers)! In contrast, if someone forgoes a high-paying job in order to work in a more pleasant environment, this worker is selfishly placing his utility above the desires of others.

The market doesn't deal in "material" goods so much as *exchangeable* goods (and services). To the extent that the market provides ever greater quantities of exchangeable goods, it lowers their marginal utilities and hence raises the relative importance of *nonexchangeable* goods.

10. Back to the Jungle?

Many allege that the unregulated market would implement Social Darwinism in which the strong destroyed the weak. Yet this biological analogy overlooks the criterion of "fitness" in a marketplace: serving the wishes of the consumers. Those who feel the market has been too harsh with particular people are free to set up assistance programs.

11. Power and Coercion

A. "Other Forms of Coercion": Economic Power

Those who claim that government must counterbalance private economic power (such as that wielded by an employer) mischaracterize the situation. If an employer refuses to hire a worker, he is merely exercising his property right; i.e., he is simply refraining from exchanging his money for the worker's labor services. If the government can justly use violence to compel an exchange, then the individual worker would likewise be entitled to take the employer's money through force.

B. Power Over Nature and Power Over Man

References to "robber barons" and "economic royalists" are inappropriate. The market economy is a positive sum game, in which there is a harmony of interests. As man's power *over nature* grows, civilization develops. Yet a rise in one man's power *over another man* retards growth and represents a net loss.

12. The Problem of Luck

It is true that the uncertainty of the future allows some to prosper and others to suffer through "luck." However, this alone does not prove that market outcomes are unfair. After all, it is possible that all of the rich are actually earning less than their true DMVPs, while all of the poor are currently enjoying

Chapter 6: Antimarket Ethics: A Praxeological Critique 235

excellent luck and really would be paid much less if entrepreneurs had correctly forecasted the future.

13. The Traffic-Manager Analogy

In a free society all roads would be privately owned, and the profit-maximizing rules would be established on them. It is a complete *non sequitur* to argue that the need for traffic regulations somehow proves the necessity of government.

14. Over- and Underdevelopment

The critics contradict themselves when it comes to "backward" countries. On the one hand, they say that advanced economies are now so complex that they require planning. On the other hand, they maintain that underdeveloped nations need the guiding hand of the State in order to catch up to the West.

15. The State and the Nature of Man

It is common to observe that man is a social animal and hence requires a government. Yet this conflates *society* with the *State*. If private legal and police services are indeed feasible, then society can flourish without coercive government.

16. Human Rights and Property Rights

It is pointless to argue that "human rights" should trump property rights, for *all* rights are ultimately property rights. Moreover, they are property rights *of humans*. (If a man has a property right in a chair, it is not the chair that possesses the right, but the human being.)

The classic examples of crying fire in a public theater etc. can all be resolved by a specification of property rights. There is no need to weigh one abstract right against another; it is all a matter of contracts.

APPENDIX:
Professor Oliver on Socioeconomic Goals

A. The Attack on Natural Liberty

Oliver rightly criticizes watered-down versions of laissez-faire, but he fails to seriously consider the Rothbardian position. Many of Oliver's alleged inconsistencies in the doctrine are due to his straw man construction.

B. The Attack on Freedom of Contract

Oliver again dismisses the radical position of unfettered freedom of contract, and focuses his attacks on versions that are either patently silly or are marred by unnecessary and confusing caveats. Rothbard provides a sound formulation of freedom-of-contract that deals with Oliver's concerns and is fully consistent with unbridled laissez-faire.

C. The Attack on Income According to Earnings

Oliver wrongly states the position he wishes to attack as, "A man acquires a right to income which he himself creates." Rothbard offers a better formulation as, "A man acquires a right to the *property* that he himself creates." Oliver goes on to question marginal productivity theory, but this is entirely irrelevant to the ethical problem of property rights: When a capitalist employer hires someone's labor, the employer is the just owner of the resulting product.

Chapter 6: Antimarket Ethics: A Praxeological Critique   237

Notable Contributions

• Beyond using value-free economics to rule out ethical goals that rest upon false beliefs concerning a market economy, Rothbard explicitly relies on praxeology (p. 1298) when explaining why movements *toward* an impossible goal are also objectionable. Although most people would likely agree with this position, it would be hard to justify (to those for whom it was not self-evident) without the praxeological argument.

• Rothbard's defense of market "monopoly" in the case of Crusoe and Friday (p. 1299) is particularly clever.

Technical Matters

1. By an "existential criticism" (e.g., p. 1298), Rothbard means a criticism that involves a value judgment, but also relies on beliefs about how the world works. Thus if someone criticizes the free market because it leads to famine, this involves the value judgment that "starvation is bad." However, there is no need to argue over ethics, because praxeology demonstrates that the free market does *not* lead to famine.

2. When Rothbard criticizes utilitarianism (p. 1304), he does not necessarily mean the doctrine of Jeremy Bentham, but rather has in mind a *consequentalist ethics* of the type espoused by Ludwig von Mises. In this conception, ultimate value judgments really are "arbitrary" in the sense that no one could possibly prove them to be correct or incorrect. However, Mises thought that (coupled with praxeology and other value-free sciences) rational individuals would realize that their (admittedly subjective) goals would best be satisfied by obeying the standard tenets of morality. For example, to the extent that the vast majority prefer wealth to poverty, health to sickness, and so on, then they would understand that they had to refrain from murder and theft.

3. When Rothbard declares, "There is but one way that morality can spread from the enlightened to the unenlightened—and that is by rational persuasion" (p. 1305), he is not advocating pacifism. He would think it perfectly acceptable for a private agency to use force, say, to stop a man from killing his neighbor. However, the point of such force would not be to create a moral man, but rather to prevent a crime.

Chapter 6: Antimarket Ethics: A Praxeological Critique   239

Study Questions

1. Does Rothbard think the end justifies the means? (p. 1298)

2. Name three typical objections to the market, and give Rothbard's responses (pp. 1299–1300).

3. Why does Rothbard say that "each man should have X" is a much clearer rule than "all men should be equal in X"? (p. 1312)

4. What was Clara Dixon Davidson's observation on Herbert Spencer's famous Law of Equal Freedom? (p. 1312, fn 13)

5. Rothbard claims (p. 1324) that the market's increased output of exchangeable goods would foster the opposite of "material" values. Give an example.

6. Explain Nock's distinction between social and State power (pp. 1331–32).

7. How does gambling fit into Rothbard's discussion of luck? (pp. 1333–34)

8. In a free society, how would people settle the conflict between movie stars' desire for privacy and the tabloid customers' desire to see candid photos? (p. 1339)

240   *Study Guide to Man, Economy, and State with Power and Market*

9. Oliver claims that natural rights connote a concept of property consisting in "things" rather than abstract "rights." What is Rothbard's response? (pp. 1342–43)

10. What does Rothbard say in response to Oliver's contention that marginal productivity cannot be applied within a corporation? (p. 1353)

CHAPTER 7

CONCLUSION: ECONOMICS AND PUBLIC PROPERTY

Chapter Outline

1. Economics: Its Nature and Its Uses

Economics is a science that provides us with true laws of cause and effect. It tells us that *if* we know A is true, *then* we conclude that B must also be true. Even though the logical implication is necessarily true (if our deductions are free of error), the conclusion B is only true when the initial assumption A is satisfied.

On an unhampered market, the economic theorist is of little use to the businessperson. However, in a regulated market, the economist can often provide insight because he understands the effects of intervention. The economist can say what will happen when the demand for butter increases, but this is of no use to the dairy farmer, who needs to know *if* the demand for butter will change. But such conditional laws are useful in public policy debates, because *if* the minimum law will change is precisely what the citizens can (indirectly) determine.

2. Implicit Moralizing: The Failures of Welfare Economics

The mainstream economist often smuggles dubious value judgments into his allegedly scientific work. Beyond this,

241

242   *Study Guide to Man, Economy, and State with Power and Market*

mainstream economists often openly announce the ethical goal—such as "equality"—and then design policies to approach it. They are wrong for thinking that their role as mere advisor is still neutral, for by helping others achieve the goal, they implicitly endorse it.

3. Economics and Social Ethics

Even the *Wertfrei* economist can play a role in public policy questions. First, using only praxeology, he can rule out meaningless or conceptually impossible ethical goals championed by others, and he can also refute popular objections to the market that rely on false propositions. Second, the *Wertfrei* economist can explain all of the myriad consequences of government intervention and of complete socialism, and contrast these effects with the description of a free market economy.

4. The Market Principle and the Hegemonic Principle

There are only two methods of social relations, the market versus the hegemonic principle. The difference can be summarized in the following table:

Chapter 7: Conclusion: Economics and Public Property 243

SOME CONSEQUENCES OF:

THE MARKET PRINCIPLE	THE HEGEMONIC PRINCIPLE
individual freedom	coercion
general mutual benefit (maximized social utility)	exploitation—benefit of one group at expense of another
mutual harmony	caste conflict: war of all against all
peace	war
power of man over nature	power of man over man
most efficient satisfaction of consumer wants	disruption of want-satisfaction
economic calculation	calculational chaos
incentives for production and advance in living standards	destruction of incentives: capital consumption and regression of living standards

Notable Contributions

• Rothbard's view (p. 1362) that the economist in a mere advisory role is implicitly endorsing the goals of his or her superiors is actually fairly unorthodox. Most economists believe that, as technicians, they can inform politicians about the likely consequences of various policies, all the while maintaining their own neutrality. However, surely Rothbard's view is correct if we change the scenario to physicists and chemists working on horrible weapons for a totalitarian government.

• Rothbard even departs from Mises on the issue of ethical judgments. Mises generally assumed that, e.g., price controls only occurred because people falsely believed they would help the poor. Once economists had explained the true situation, Mises thought, the support for price controls would vanish. But as Rothbard points out (p. 1362), it is entirely possible that the rulers know the effects of their interventions and simply rank their own power higher on their scale of values than the welfare of their subjects.

Chapter 7: Conclusion: Economics and Public Property 245

Technical Matters

1. *Wertfrei* was the German term Mises often used to describe economic science. It means "value-free." This doesn't mean that the study of economics commits one to nihilism, but rather that economics *itself* is a positive (versus normative) enterprise that discovers true causal relations in the world. In the same way, medicine is value-free; one must study bacteria or cancer in a neutral way to understand them. Of course the *application* of economic or medical science necessarily involves value judgments.

2. Rothbard, unlike Mises, did not endorse Hume's famous fact/value dichotomy, often summarized by, "You can't derive an *ought* from an *is*." Rothbard thought that an objective ethics was indeed possible, and that one could legitimately argue with another's chosen values. Even so, Rothbard agrees with Mises that *economics* cannot do this.

246   *Study Guide to Man, Economy, and State with Power and Market*

Study Questions

1. Give an example of a praxeological law with a conclusion that is always true, and one with a conclusion that might not be true in a particular situation (p. 1357).

2. Give some examples of "implicit moralizing" in mainstream economics (pp. 1360–61).

3. If the economist who advises an interventionist government is endorsing their goals (p. 1362), then would an economist who explains the effects of socialism (p. 1363) still be *Wertfrei*? (p. 1363)

4. What are the three possible responses of the hypothetical director of the Office of Price Administration? Which of these is consistent with praxeology? (pp. 1364–65)

5. If the world is a complex place, where each society has a mixture of the market and hegemonic principles, isn't Rothbard's table a bit simplistic? (pp. 1365–66)

6. Why does the "mixed" society move toward one of the polar opposites of pure market or pure hegemony? (p. 1366)

7. Is a socialist community impossible? (pp. 1366–67)

Chapter 7: Conclusion: Economics and Public Property 247

8. Is a purely free economy necessarily stable? (p. 1367)

9. Why is the American farm program a "classic example" of the cumulative nature of intervention? (pp. 1367–68)

10. What does Proudhon mean by his maxim, "Liberty the Mother, not the Daughter, of Order"? (p. 1368)

INDEX

Apriorism, 1, 9
Ability-to-pay principle, 211
Absolute advantage, 18
Acceleration principle, 147
Action, 3
Advertising, 129, 160, 164
Affluence, 164
Agio. *See* Interest
Algebra, 150–51
Antitrust laws, 190, 194
Arrow-Debreu, 64
Autistic exchange, 17
Average physical product (APP), 84
Awareness, 17

Balance of payments, 32, 144
Bank/banking
    100 percent reserve, 142–43
    fractional-reserve (FRB), 142
    run, 165
Barriers to entry, 125
Barter, economy, 35
    See also Exchange, direct
Basing-point pricing, 194
Belief, 2, 4
Bentham, Jeremy, 238
Bills of exchange, 145
Böhm-Bawerk, Eugen, 9, 62, 99, 102, 115
Boom, runaway, 165
    See also Business cycle
Bribery, 196

Bureaucracy, 121, 124
Buridan's ass, 49
Business cycle, 146, 156, 164, 165
Bust. *See* Business cycle

Calculation, economic, 28, 108, 112, 113, 116, 121, 124, 125, 162
Cannan, Edwin, 169
Capacity, paradox of excess, 128–29
Capital goods (factors of production), 4, 5, 7, 82, 85, 104
    complementary, 7
Capital, structure of, 163, 164
    working, 104
Capitalists, 32, 59, 70
Capitalization, 40, 46
Caplan, Bryan, 185
Cardinality, 6, 51
Cartel/cartels, 121, 124–25
    as similar to mergers and corporations, 124
    one big, 125
    compulsory, 190, 192
Cash balance, 32, 135, 137
Catallactics, 28
Chamberlin, Edward Hastings, 129
Chaos. *See* Calculation, economic
Charity, poverty and, 233
Child labor laws, 190, 193
Choice, 1
Circular flow diagram, 34, 77
Clark, John Bates, 9

249

Clearinghouses, 144
Clemence, Richard Vernon, 79
Coinage, 149, 197
Coincidence of wants, 27, 29
Collective goods. *See* Public goods
Command posts, 162
Comparative advantage, 16, 18
Competition, monopoly, 128
    perfect, 122, 128
Competitive price, 122
    See also Monopoly/monopolies/
        monopolistic, price
Complementarity, 46
Condition, general, 4
Conflict, 162
Conscription, 190, 193
Conservation laws, 190, 195
Consumer/consumers'
    sovereignty, 121, 123
    "surplus," 43
Consumption, function, 147
    See also Government spending
Convertibility, 7
Copyrights, 129
Corporations
    limited liability, 196–97
Cost/costs, 45, 56, 58
    alleged distinction between pro-
        duction and selling, 129
    of living, 113
    theory of prices, 214
    transaction, 129
Court of final opinion, 176
Credit expansion, 156, 164–65
    See also Inflation, monetary
Crime. *See* Intervention

Deadweight loss, 131
Defense services, 175–76, 213

Demand, 16, 19, 42, 132
    exchange, for money, 137, 150
    law of, 116
    reservation, 21, 110, 137
    speculative, 139
    to hold, 20
Democracy, 182, 193, 220, 224, 225
    as contradictory, 223
    in two senses, 222
Department of Commerce, 220, 223,
    225
Development, over- and under-, 235
Diminishing marginal utility, law of,
    6, 47
Discounting, 84
Distribution, 61
    production and, 108, 113
Division-of-labor, 15, 18, 206
Doody, 79
Draft. *See* Conscription

Economics, 3, 9, 169, 241
Economies of scale, 121, 124
Economists, 241
Economizing, 4
Economy
    Evenly Rotating (ERE), 11, 55,
        57, 60, 64, 71, 76, 82, 113
    progressing, 94, 98, 100
    retrogressing, 94, 98, 100
    stationary, 94
Elasticity
    of demand, 20, 132
    of supply, 25
Employment, full, 111, 141
Ends, 4, 47
Entrepreneurship, 2, 4, 95–96
    self-employment and, 112
Envy, 182, 185
Equality, 230, 232
    before the law, 210

Index 251

Equilibrium, 47, 104
    macro, 140
    price, 16, 19, 42
Error, 95
Ethics
    antimarket, 229–38
    consequentialist, 238
    social, 242
Ex ante utility, 45, 155, 157, 181
Ex post utility, 45, 155, 157, 182
Exchange, 1
    direct, 15, 27, 41
    equation of, 145
    indirect, 15, 27
    interlocal, 144
Exchange-value, 15, 18
Existential criticism, 238
Externalities, positive and negative, 166–67

Factor incomes, 85
Factors of production. *See* Capital goods (factors of production)
Fetter, Frank A., 11
Fisher, Irving, 141, 149, 207, 215
Fixed proportions, 90
Franchises, 196
Free markets. *See* Market, unhampered
Freedom, 230
    of the consumer, 125
    of contract, 236

Galbraith, John Kenneth, 164
George, Henry, 110
Georgism, 204
Gold, 28, 49
Goods, 4
    consumers', 4
    durable, 46

exchangeable (nonexchangeable), 233
Giffen, 116
producers'
    See also Capital goods (factors of production)
Government, 155, 157, 166, 181, 235
    borrowing, 166
    limited, 176
    productive contributions of, spending, 156, 161
    provision of defense services, 175
    resource-using activities of, 162
    run on a "business basis," 162, 221
    spending, 156, 159, 205, 219, 221
    "voluntary," 182
Growth, 163

Hayek, Friedrich August, 116
Hegemony, 17, 157, 242
Hire price. *See* Rental price
Hoarding, 135, 140
Homesteading, 22
Human
    nature, 232, 235
    rights, 235–36
Hume, David, 225, 245
Hutt, William Harold, 123, 130, 147
Hyperinflation, 165

Immigration, restrictions on, 190, 193, 197
Incentives, 169, 206
Incidence. *See* Taxes/taxation, incidence of
Income, gross, 108, 112
Indispensability, 64–65
Individualism, methodological, 2, 3
Inflation, monetary, 156, 161, 164
    price, 165

See also Credit expansion; Hyperinflation

Innovation, 146, 195.
   See also Technique
Insurance, 163, 176
Integration, vertical, 71, 113
Interest, 55, 56, 59, 103
   compounding of, 78
   market (nominal or loan) rate of, 94, 150, 170
   entrepreneurial component in market rate of, 100
   "natural rate" of, 170
   pure rate of, 69, 72, 74–75
   purchasing-power and terms-of-trade components in the rate of, 141
Intertemporal utility comparisons, 43
Intervention, 155, 157, 181
   autistic, 155, 157, 181
   binary, 155, 157, 159, 181, 203–16, 219–25
   triangular, 155, 157, 158, 181, 189–99
Investment, 7, 100, 102
   gross, 70
   net, 96, 104
   trusts, 79
   See also Savings

Joint-stock company, 75
Judicial services. *See* Defense services
Just price, 204, 209
Justice, canons of, in taxation, 209

Keynes, John Maynard, 107, 111, 116, 150
Keynesianism, 140, 147, 161, 224
Kinsella, Stephan, 130
Knight, Frank, 9, 87, 101
Kuznets, Simon, 220, 223, 225

Labor, 5, 7, 109
   supply curve of, 107, 110, 116
Land, 5, 82, 85, 89
   scarcity of, relative to labor, 109
   supply curve of, 107
Law Code, 176, 178
Laws. *See* Diminishing marginal utility, law of; Returns, law of; One price, law of; Demand, law of
Lebensraum, 197
Leisure, 7, 110, 116, 216
Libertarianism, 178
Licensing, 190, 192, 199
Liquidity, 79
Location, spatial relations and, 113
Log-rolling, 24
Loss. *See* Profit, loss and
Luck, 234–35
Lutz, Friedrich August, 79

Management, as labor, 109
Marginal physical product (MPP), 81, 84, 87, 110
Marginal product, 7, 11
Marginal utility, 2, 6, 18, 45, 47
Marginal value product (MVP), 81, 83, 85, 87
   discounted (DMVP), 81, 83, 108, 111
Marginalism. *See* Marginal utility
Market/markets, black, 189, 191
   producers' loan, 74–75
   time, 73
   unhampered (free), 16, 22, 166, 175, 241
Marshall, Alfred, 60, 63, 115
Materialism, selfish, 233
Means, 4–5, 47
   See also Goods
Medieval society, 230, 232

Index

253

Medium of exchange, 27, 31
  See also Money
Menger, Carl, 9, 34, 35, 36, 63
Military. *See* Defense services
Minimum wage laws, 194
Mises, Ludwig von, 9–10, 23, 40, 49,
  62, 64, 102, 115, 116, 225, 238, 244,
  245
Models, 36
Molinari, Gustave de, 177
Money, 27–28, 135–48
  as measure of value, 136, 146
  certificates (substitutes), 142
  changes in, relation, 138
  demand for, 135, 165
  exchange demand for, 137, 150
  expenditures, 32
  implications of the emergence of,
    31
  in the broader sense, 142
  income, 32
  marginal utility of, 33, 43, 39
  non-neutrality of, 136, 143
  proper, 142
  purchasing power of (PPM), 39,
    40, 41, 43–44, 135, 136, 137,
    138
  quasi, 145
  secular influences on the demand
    for, 139
  stability of, 146
  stock (supply), 73–74, 135–36,
    137, 138, 142
  unit of, 32
  warehousing, 142
  See also Regression theorem
Monopoly/monopolies/monopolistic,
  122, 126–27, 131, 169, 189, 192,
  196, 237
  competition, 128
  price, 122, 126–27, 169, 199

profits, 126, 169
unions as, 122, 127
Morality, 229, 231, 238
Multiplier, Keynesian, 147

Natural resources, depletion of, 86
Nonaggression axiom, 176, 178

Oligopoly. *See* Monopoly
Oliver, Henry M., Jr., 236
One price, law of, 20, 41, 108
Orders of production, 5
Ordinality, 6, 51
Overpopulation, 197
Ownership, 220, 221, 222

Pacifism, 238
Pareto optimality, 185
Patents, 129, 195
Perks, wage rates and, 111
Pessimism, 10
Planning, central, 46
  See also Socialism
Police. *See* Defense services
Post-income demanders, 74
Power, economic (over nature), 234
  See also Hegemony
Praxeology, 1, 3, 9, 169, 229, 231, 237
Price/prices, 16, 18–19, 61
  calculation and, 112
  controls, 155, 157, 189, 191, 244
  costs and, 107, 112
  indices, 146
  multiform, 129
  nominal, 40
  See also Monopoly/monopolies/
    monopolistic, price
Producer "surplus," 43

Product control, 158, 169, 189, 191–92
Productivity/production, 70
    period of, 5
    physical, 99
    structure of, 9, 73
    See also Marginal physical product
Profit, 55, 93, 95, 103
    accounting, 103
    economic, 103
    general "rate of," 102
    loss and, 93, 95, 103–04
    money, 103
Prohibition, 189, 191
    partial, 192
Propaganda, 176, 178
Property rights, 175, 196, 230, 235
Psychic, profit, 25
    revenue, 1, 25, 33
Public goods, 166
Public ownership, 163, 219–20, 222
Purchasing power, excess, 161
    parity (PPP), 136, 145
Purpose, 1, 3

Quality, 192
Quantity demanded or supplied, 19

Reason, 238
Regression theorem, 40, 44
Relative advantage. *See* comparative advantage
Rental price, 40, 46
Rents, 11, 60, 86, 107, 109
    net, 109
Reproducibility, 11
Return/returns, gross, 11
    law of, 7, 84
    net, 62
    See also Interest

Reverse valuation, 15, 17, 24
Ricardo, David, 113
Rights. *See* Property rights
Risk, 94, 101
Robinson Crusoe economics, 9
Rolph, Earl, 87
Roundaboutness, 9

Sacrifice theory, 211
Safety, 192
Saleability. *See* Marketability
Sam's Club, 131–32
Samuelson, Paul Anthony, 62
Saving, 7, 100
    net, 104
    paradox of, 102
Scarcity, 4
School, compulsory, 190, 193
Schumpeter, Joseph, 62, 76, 146
Security, 230, 232
Self-interest, knowledge of, 231
Shifting, 160
Shortage, 19–20, 155, 158, 189, 191
Silver, 28
Slavery, 17, 109
Smith, Adam, 209
Social Darwinism, 230, 233
Social Security, 163
Socialists/socialism, 163, 219, 222
    calculation problem and, 108, 113, 162
    democratic, 220, 223
    "market," 116
Society, 235
Sovereignty, individual, 121, 123
Specialization, 15, 18, 20, 21
Specificity, 7, 57, 58, 81, 83, 89
Speculation, 4, 16, 50
    withholding of land for, 110
State, the. *See* Government
Stationary state, 9

Index 255

See also Economy, Evenly Rotating (ERE)
Status society, 232
Stock, total, 6, 20
Subjectivity, 12, 15, 63
Subsidies, 161, 219, 221
Substitutability, 46
Supply, 16, 19, 42
Surplus, 19, 155, 158, 189, 191
Synchronization, 9

Tariffs, 190, 193
Tax/taxes/taxation, 156, 203–16
    consumers, 205
    consumption, 203, 207
    corporate income, 203, 206–07
    "double," 206
    flat, 156, 159
    general sales, 160, 205
    head (equal), 156, 159, 212
    incidence, 160, 169, 203, 205–09, 214
    income, 159, 203, 205, 206–07, 216
    land value (ground rent), 160, 204, 209
    neutral, 156, 159, 210–12
    on accumulated capital, 204, 207
    on bequests and gifts, 208
    on individual wealth, 208
    on wages, 206
    partial excise, 206
    payers, 205
    progressive, 204, 208
    See also Tariffs
Technique, 99, 146
    See also Innovation
Time, 2, 4, 9
    maturing, 5

preference, 2, 6, 70, 72, 76, 79, 159, 163, 195
working, 5
Traffic-manager analogy to government, 235
Transfer payments. *See* Subsidies
Typology of intervention, 155, 157, 168, 181, 184, 198

U.S.A., 219, 222
U.S.S.R., 219, 222
Uncertainty, 2, 101, 114, 235
Unemployment, 111
    government, benefits, 190, 194
Unions, 109
    compulsory, 122, 127, 194
Unit (of a good), 6
Use-value, 15, 18, 21
Utility, 182
    See also Ex ante utility; *Ex post* utility

Value judgments, 238
Value scales, 1, 42, 72
Value, 11, 48
Violence, institutionalized. *See* Government

Wages, 107, 109, 110–11, 112
    real, 116–17, 141
Wagner-Taft-Hartley Act, 194
Walrasian analysis, 116
Welfare, economic, 168
    economics, 241–42
    See also Utility
Wertfrei, 242, 245

Zones of indeterminacy, 61, 122, 127